The Black Mountain Letters

JONATHAN C. CREASY

The Black Mountain Letters

Poems & Essays

DALKEY ARCHIVE PRESS

Library of Congress Cataloging-in-Publication Data

Names: Creasy, Jonathan C., author.
Title: The Black Mountain letters : poems and essays / Jonathan C. Creasy.
Description: 1st ed. | Victoria, TX : Dalkey Archive Press, 2016.
Identifiers: LCCN 2016010909 | ISBN 9781564789297 (pbk. : alk. paper)
Subjects: LCSH: Black Mountain College (Black Mountain, N.C.)
Classification: LCC PS3603.R436 A6 2016 | DDC 818/.6--dc23
LC record available at https://lccn.loc.gov/2016010909

Partially funded by a grant by the Illinois Arts Council, a state agency

www.dalkeyarchive.com

Victoria, TX / McLean, IL / Dublin

Dalkey Archive Press publications are, in part, made possible through the
support of the University of Houston-Victoria and its programs in creative
writing, publishing, and translation.

Cover: Art by Katherine O'Shea

Printed on permanent/durable acid-free paper

Kneel to intellect in our work
Chaos cast cold intellect back

Susan Howe

My Imaginary Genius, by Astrid Kaemmerling

(in correspondence with the author)

To the Reader

This book is a collage text of poetry and prose made out of my work on Black Mountain College. It grows out of correspondence with Susan Howe, Mary Emma Harris, Astrid Kaemmerling, and affinities with Charles Olson, Robert Creeley, Robert Duncan, John Cage, William Carlos Williams, and many others. During the period of my research and writing, 2011–2015, I visited Black Mountain, North Carolina on many occasions. Other locations colour the writing: Dublin, New York City, Paris, and Berlin. Black Mountain College intensified the sense of place of those who were there. My own interactions with Black Mountain – the land, the college, works produced on its grounds and in its shadow – continue to have an impact on my sense of the world and the word.

My mother – Lynette Jean Creasy – suffered catastrophic heart failure at a wedding party outside Paris, with a glass of champagne still in her hand. On July 9, 2013, she died in Cergy-Pontoise Hospital. The work I have done during this period is shaped by that sudden loss.

This book is a new form of expository elegy.

I dedicate it to her, and to all friends and family – real and imagined.

Songbirds of Cergy

for my mother

Ended as you ought to be,
pâté en croûte –
friends, wine, & wedding –

all-together painless.

A song,
you song-less bird,
without throat to carry.

Happy for others
to do your singing for you –

Rattle we heard
most of an hour
    until we could no longer.

& then, all the endless days passing.

You must have known
songbirds of Cergy,
their wise music knowing;

    it has brought us all-together.

Ended as you ought to be,
in these hills beyond Paris –

two sons, husband,
    legend of classroom legacy.

I've been told your French was strong.
Only to have heard you speak it.

Lines, for now, that cannot feel-out
                              the unfeeling.

We eat – we drink – we rest:
all-together singing; knowing.

A song, as a bird's, a whisper, that rattle –
Over & over, in nightly visitation.

By the brokenness of his composition the poet makes himself master of a certain weapon which he could possess himself of in no other way. The speed of the emotions is sometimes such that thrashing about in a thin exaltation or despair many matters are touched but not held, more often broken by the contact.

William Carlos Williams ('The Dr.'),
Kora in Hell: Improvisations (1920)

Asheville

[archive]

Black Mountain was freedom.

And within that freedom I and others developed a discipline in [. . .] writing that involved listening and seeing with such continuous intensity it became my way of life. As much an influence on me today, and every day, as it ever was. Black Mountain was not something you grew out of. Like freedom, you grew into it.

People who didn't go to the school will never understand that like freedom, the school was atemporal, which gave it its transparent character [. . .].

The story is within the crystal, not without. All the interviewing of former students and faculty, including a book and exhibition of our works of art, are but shallow reminders, dim reflections. It is too bad, and may seem unfair, but so Black Mountain was, and if you *weren't there you will never know, or understand.*

Unless you create it. That's the catch. If you never were there (or were!), and write it, you'll have to create it [. . .]. So, in the original Happening, as Mary Harris documents, Cage's stepladder, radio, dogs and dancers production at school [. . .]. Cage created it. So too must it be written.

Fielding Dawson, *The Black Mountain Book* (1990)

Studies Building, Lake Eden, Black Mountain College
Courtesy of the Western Regional Archives,
State Archives of North Carolina

If one knows anything about Black Mountain College, it is probably a list of names – a roll call of the mid-twentieth-century avant-garde: Josef and Anni Albers, Franz Kline, Robert Motherwell, John Cage, Merce Cunningham, Robert Rauschenberg, Ray Johnson, Ruth Asawa, M. C. Richards, Lou Harrison, Willem and Elaine de Kooning, Cy Twombly, Paul Goodman, Charles Olson, Robert Duncan, Robert Creeley, Buckminster Fuller, and the list goes on. But this is only part of the story. To view the life of the college only through its most famous names is to underestimate the task set by its founders and limit its legacy in educational and artistic practices today. To paraphrase Martin Duberman, we must cease to conflate notoriety with existence.

Founded in 1933 in the mountains of Western North

Carolina and dissolved by 1957, Black Mountain College lasted a short time under extraordinary circumstances. It was established on the principles of John Dewey's progressive education philosophy and placed the arts at the centre of a general curriculum. The college went through at least three distinct phases, led in turn by three powerful personalities: classicist John Andrew Rice, painter Josef Albers, and poet Charles Olson. Though it is primarily known now as a remote and rural escape for artists who went on to shape the postwar cultural landscape, Black Mountain must also be understood as a daring departure from conventional forms of higher education, a revision of our usual ways of seeing the world. This idealistic, utopian experiment in education folded because of financial pressures and petty in-fighting, at once offering encouragement but also warning to those who see today's systems of education as exclusionary, debased, and fundamentally removed from the aspirations of civil society. The art – Black Mountain's most profound legacy – lives on in institutions around the world, summoning voices of the past.

Insistent imaginations prevail upon our own.

July 20, 2013

Dear Jonathan,

How horrible. Was it a heart attack? Your mother was SO young! As you know, I have been through this and you will feel the terrible shock for a long time. My father died when he was 60 and I was 29. He was thought to be in perfect health and yet a heart attack killed him in an hour. I know the clarity and the motivation that follows in the wake of such a shock. In the case of my father he acted as a sort of muse for work that I did for years after.

When and if your parent dies so young and so swiftly, you remember them at the height of their powers, still young; none of the decay of old age. This has its good side because your remembrance only goes that far.

Your elegy is beautiful. Elegies do provide comfort, the writing of them, I am sure there will be more to come because all of your writing will be somehow connected to the shock of her absence for some time. Having spent so long on Stevens's last poems and even Yeats's uncomforting 'Cuchulain Comforted,' the mystery and wonder of the cries of birds and their language-music we can never understand is a tribute, answer, and call.

All the best, and with hopes you can get a bit of rest during August.

Susan

Today, at exactly twelve noon, as I read
'under the flightpath, up, / wheels dip,
flaps down, a steady waver in the great /
machine where jets make landfall and go on'
Streaming jets slowed the graying sky
out the window, Mountjoy eyed askance,
the destitute table destined in its form
to outlast my Maturity. Given the stakes,
I repeat *I prefer not to*, exercise will, & move on.

Great deeds looking back into history are
anarchisms. Stay with me. They grow from
ground up. This is not original. Years,
decades maybe before we break the surface
but stating here, in no uncertain terms, our
purpose. 'No novel incoming of bare abstract
form.' Just patience, same will as ever
to change, with our breathless sighs the sight
departing Dublin airport at 5 o'clock in the morning.

```
measure up.
            No eyes or ears left          is a protest that rises from the,
      to do their own doings              is rooted in, keen sense of what
eye and ear need be.  Sights and soundings.  "the attention, and/ the care."

   It is enough.  Enough surely.  The reader can put it all together: the "by
ear", "be played by .../ the ear", "she looks / as the best of my people look/
in one direction", "the hands he'd purposely allowed to freeze to the oars",
"eyed (with a like eye)", "look right straight down into yr pages", "polis is
/ eyes", "that those who are sharp haven't got that way / by pushing their
limits", "his eyes / as a gull's are", "by gift? bah  by love of self? try it
by god? ask . / the bean sandwich", "As hands are put to the eyes' commands",
"a man's hands, / as his eyes, / can get sores)", "(each finger) their own
lives' acts", "to have a heart",
   And I feel that way
   that the likeness is to nature's,
   not to these tempestuous
   events.                              The major address of the poem is to
what the act need be--to
   felicity
   resulting from life of acitivity in accordance with
              2
On the level of reference, the gain from Whitman's address to his cosmic body
to Olson's address to "The waist of a lion / for a man to move properly" is
immense.
```

Scrap of a letter from Robert Duncan to Charles Olson,
May 17, 1955

Charles Olson Research Collection
Archives and Special Collections at the Thomas J. Dodd Research Center
University of Connecticut Libraries

[Black Mountain, NC]
Tuesday may whatever it is
[9 May 1950]

my dear robert creeley:

this is going to be a note, only, to tell you i have been on the road for ten days, and will write you the moment i am back at my desk

but i want you to know how very glad i am that you saw Morning News, and that goes for y & x, and the new two, too it is fine

it did startle me, you speak of education, & plan to speak up: nothing could be truer, when poets are the only pedagogues

i don't think you could know that you would catch me, with yr letter, when I was at Alabama College doing a speech on verse and showing Cagli drawings And now i am here at this little hotbox of education, to do the same i shall try to put down something on education for you: USE, it is the use they make of us

    above all things resist, to be sick at heart: we are forward, and it is such gratification, that you are ready to go with me

love,
   olson[1]

Thoughts After Olson

Show me archaeologist
    & cartographer,
backlit flicker of shadow, as in the cave
    of my own mind –
Where what's initial, all that is
    ever-becoming
                    or possible;
setting out with each moment,
without *sense of an ending:*

'"walking," the unremitting curiosity
    without which [. . .]
            there can be no literature'
&c

IMAGO MUNDI
    our sacred order,
& all the lyrics made classical
before the last grain's sifted.

We live in a 'late era'
    I've heard it said.

For the first-people
        more might have been
                apparent.

But we – the livers & liars – left our philosophies,
        our theologies,
washed them in blood
        & buried dogmas in invented order:
war; *love*; *literature* & so on.

When breathed into officious
lungs, the breath God gave
                to our animation,

a plan to dwell in infancy
        till – subtly – we were outwitted.

In a decision reached by the American Association of University Professors, it was determined that at Rollins College in Florida John Andrew Rice sought

> to bring students to substitute, in place of assumptions accepted through tradition or convention, personal convictions reached through reflection; and that he did this chiefly, not by lecturing, but by a searching and skillful use of the Socratic dialogue.[2]

These remarks came in an appeals hearing initiated by Rice after he was fired from Rollins by president Hamilton Holt. Holt found Rice to be a disruption to the college: he was arrogant, it was charged, insensitive to conventions of gender roles and general propriety; some of his students complained that Rice bullied them, that they were publicly humiliated. Rice had apparently displayed 'obscene' pictures on the walls of his Greek Civilization class, and had excoriated fellow faculty for what he saw as their intellectual and pedagogical weaknesses. He was even charged with indecency on account of his preferred swimming attire.

The AAUP hearings vindicated Rice, though he left Rollins all the same. This was 1933, with the Great Depression well underway. Rice found himself out of work, while his career-long reputation as iconoclast and pedagogical searcher left him no option or interest in pursuing work at a conventional institution.

In his book *Black Mountain College: An Exploration in Community* (1972), Martin Duberman writes,

> Rice hated what he called the 'top sergeants' in teaching, of whom he took Thomas Arnold of Rugby to be the exemplar: 'He was a builder of empire builders, and a destroyer of men, for he forces them into the mold of the immutable past.' Teachers like Arnold, Rice felt, had a deep distrust of learning, even while using it as a weapon to keep their students in line.[3]

That summer of 1933, Rice helped establish one of the most vital experiments in education, art, and living ever attempted in the United States. As location, he and his small band chose the mountains of North Carolina, far away from the artistic centres of New York, Chicago, Los Angeles, and the great cities of Europe. The remove afforded artists, teachers, and inventors the space and time to experiment in ways they could not possibly have managed elsewhere. In the beginning, great obstacles were set before Rice and his idealist companions (some of whom had left Rollins in protest or had their positions terminated by Holt for supporting Rice). Most of the twenty-odd students in Black Mountain's first class followed Rice from Rollins. Later in BMC's history, Rice's reputation was tarnished and then rehabilitated. For better or worse, he stands as an embodiment of Black Mountain's successes and failures, its vast ambitions and limited means.

In the throes of the Great Depression, with the economic foundation of the country bottomed-out, space emerged for experimentation across fields and without official sanction. In *The Arts at Black Mountain College* (1987), Mary Emma Harris writes,

> Despite the unemployment and financial hardship, the Great Depression gave rise to a garden of utopian ventures, some ephemeral, some enduring. The collapse of the financial system brought disillusionment with the existing political, economic, and social order.[4]

'Rice had often discussed the "ideal college" in his Athenian Civilization class,' Harris continues, 'and he seized the opportunity to implement his concepts.' After a national search for money and grounds, on August 24, 1933, a lease was signed with the YMCA Blue Ridge Assembly in Black Mountain, North Carolina, fifteen miles from Asheville. For $4,500 per year, Rice and his associates could run whatever experimental college they wished up until the summer months, when again the campus would be taken over by Christian summer conventions. With a $10,000 seed grant from J. Malcolm Forbes, Rice enlisted luminaries in United States academic, artistic, and financial life including Thomas Whitney Surette, director of the Concord Summer School of Music, John R. P. French, head of the Cambridge School of Weston, and Henry Allen Moe, secretary of the John Simon Guggenheim Memorial Foundation, to help found his idyllic experiment in learning.

The school's original incorporation certificate from the State of North Carolina, issued August 19, 1933, reads in part,

> The school is a place where coeds 'may receive instruction in those branches of learning which will aid in qualifying them for honorably and effectively discharging their obligations to society and their duties as citizens.'[5]

The philosopher and education theorist John Dewey influenced this stance; he saw education as the process by which able citizens of democracy are created. Rice had a personal relationship with Dewey, who acted as a close advisor to BMC and visited Rice on campus. Dewey argues,

> unless [the] end is placed in the context of services rendered to others, skills gained will be put to an egoistic and selfish use, and may be employed as means of a trained shrewdness in which one person gets the better of others. Too often, indeed, the schools, through reliance upon the spur of competition and bestowing of special honors and prizes, only build up and strengthen the disposition that makes an individual when he leaves school employ his special talents and superior skill to outwit his fellows without respect for the welfare of others.[6]

Dewey's argument is common in the progressive education movement he shaped. At Black Mountain, however, even Dewey's authoritative pronouncements were subject to question and criticism. Power was given to those who in a traditional academic setting would have had very little, as bitterly evidenced in the Rollins blowup. Instead of a board of trustees, Black Mountain was administered and directed by faculty and students. Quaker-style meetings were held to draw out consensus, a process that could be painfully tedious. Above all, a commitment to democracy guided Black Mountain's policies.

In the 1940s, BMC moved from the rented grounds of the Blue Ridge Assembly to a purchased plot of land at nearby Lake Eden. The campus sits at the foot of the mountains, with buildings scattered at the lake's edges and the college farm spread out just above. All of the elements were in place in this more permanent location, which many members of the community hoped would be self-sustaining and secure. However, Rice saw this move, especially the purchase of property, as a grave mistake (a sentiment later echoed by Olson). Rice believed the college should travel light; it should be able to pick up and move when necessary, without debts. (He also had very little interest in maintaining the farm. The inherent values of manual labour were often debated at Black Mountain, although the farm served an absolutely integral function for the community and was the strongest link between the college and the conservative town of Black Mountain, NC.)

In the context of the Depression, with the many wandering and hungry jobless, an itinerant notion of education had appeal and a good deal of validity, particularly for an institution resolutely without endowment. The move to Lake Eden also signalled a move toward the later character of Black Mountain as an arts institute rather than a progressive college and intentional community. However, the foundation built by Rice and his reading of Dewey never entirely faded. To understand Black Mountain's importance and the insistence of its legacy, one must realize its goals and effects outside the world of avant-garde arts. It started with the belief that, as Dewey writes, 'To bring to the consciousness of the coming generation something of the potential significance of the life of to-day, to transmute it from outward fact into intelligent perception, is the first step in the creation of culture.'[7] In commitment to this ideal, Black Mountain initiated students, faculty, and indeed the great artists associated with it toward what Rice called 'a grammar of the art of living.'

By the time Olson took over in the 1950s and brought Creeley and Duncan to Black Mountain, Rice's grammar was thoroughly engrained. 'Life is preoccupation with itself,' Olson writes. And so one generation follows another.

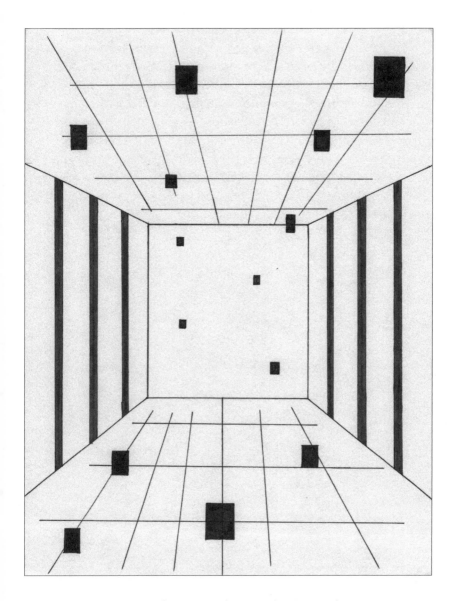

Repairing the Ravages, by Astrid Kaemmerling
(in correspondence with the author)

Bebop for Bob Creeley

I do not think

so

time never tells

when

more of the same

time –

when I was young

when I was young

three times we say

when I was young /

the world

at my feet

oh boy!

when I was young –

Lake Eden in the Winter, by Trude Guermonprez
Courtesy of the Western Regional Archives, State Archives of
North Carolina

[Littleton, NH]
Thursday
[11 May 1950]

Dear Olson,

Good to have yr letter, and good, too, mine found you where it did. So many I know are in those places now, or headed for them, because, bless us, we have to eat, etc., etc., etc. Myself, I never made the whole thing, and left 1 term short of the fatal approval. My poor mother: 20 exact yrs of saving & work, to send her lad to Hahvuhd, where the old man had went, before me, and 'its blood was green, etc., etc.' I cant face her these quiet days; we stuck to our own ways. So much for the background, etc. A tear.

So, then: good to have the fact of yr interest. I trust you for something good here. To date: have word from Emerson (golden goose) that he will give something; which, depending on time, may go in this 1st issue. We lack, there, at the moment, a center, beyond the Dr.'s shot, which being a reprint, we cant bank on for applause, certainly. I have made a few things there, but I get self-conscious writing the whole thing. With good work sur-rounded. My boy who prints this, and who, now, takes a hand (AT LAST) cant give me an exact idea as to how often or how much we can print on the press: but we will keep to it, altho the monthly appearances may be beyond it because of the job of printing & because of distribution. Should note his comment: 'the olson being all you say it is . . .' I sent him copies of the other two & the same with them. So, we're with you. Really fine things. Have tipped Emerson to yr little book and others I can get to: not only to fawn, etc., but, true, to see if I hold a lone opinion. I think not. Hope it gets around.

Inexperience, etc., make impossible an exact grip on the center at this writing. The Dr. said: ideas; yes, and I wd like to use them. But reading this morning in the UNWOBBLING PIVOT, like they say, a few simple precepts for SUCCESS. Or notes on how to prepare for the work at hand. Neither of us have had any experience in this biz; neither of us have a clear idea, at the moment, as to what bulk of frequency we can plan. My boy does say, with truth, the best thing: to plan, say, 6 issues on one center, hit it, in good critical prose, and put the good poems & stories along with it, and no attempt to make these last fit a complex PLAN, and/or, to warp them into an ambiguous relation with the criticism. In the case of yr Morning News, its purposes fall to hand, like manna. But not usual. I don't think we can get to an exact 'program' which will embrace with sincerity the present concerns of Williams, Pound, etc., etc., In the case of the Dr.: we come close because we take him to be a focus for these matters. But always, our own way, has to be it. You will know about this, certainly. Better, to make actual limits, weedings, on what might concern us and get beyond the simple broadsheet into the kind of order that a magazine wd be, even something like PR, which otherwise I wdn't like to think about. So. This 1st issue: no articulate program beyond the airing of specific concerns, here & there, and good evidence of good poetry, etc. But we have there: no 'long-range' view. I wonder if such wd best suit our purposes at the moment. Something seems necessary & yet I hate to warp or limit what development experience might get us to. All this for what concerns me at the moment. Nothing a final block. Will write you more exact information as I have it. On the education: you can plan on this being the main concern for the next issue anyhow, and maybe for the next 2 or 3 after it. Certainly not something that can be dealt with in a few mouthfuls. Think of prose for the minute. I get scared at this point. You say the poets are the only pedagogues: whatever happened to prose . . .

Am going to ask a favor, like they say, having to do, exactly, with the enclosed check for 60 c which, being an honest man,

I offer in payment for 2 copies of *Y&X* plus mailing costs, etc. Handling, like they say. Anyhow, wd you please send one of these to: E[leanor] BARON BRANDEIS UNIVERSITY, WALTHAM, MASS. It wd do her good to see this; and to, as well, MR & MRS D. BERLIN, Ario 15, Col. Roma Sur, Mexico, D.F. A stranger request: I am altogether broke at the moment & this last is my best friend, like they say, and has just got married, and wd like him to have a little book as evidence of my joy, etc. So, wd you be good enough to put an appropriate comment in the front, say, 'At length the candle's out, and now, / All that they had not done, they do. / What that is, who can tell . . .'* or what you will. Id be grateful. You will have a taste of his sentiments in this first issue; some things from a letter, which relate, strangely enough, to TS ELIOT. But you will see. Anyhow, all best to you, and will write soon again, to give you more of what's happening. You do the same.

Best,
Creeley

[*Added in pencil:*] *My wife** says: do not use this, etc. So what you will. [*Typed:*] **She went to Black Mountain, for 2 or 3 months. I visited. All I can remember 2 miles up a dirt road, all dressed up, lugging a rock-like suitcase. Pretty hopeless, then. And now?[8]

Most of the materials collected from Black Mountain College's relatively brief existence remain in the western regional branch of the North Carolina State Archives, Asheville, NC. I have made several visits to the State Archives, along with related research trips to Yale's Beinecke Rare Book & Manuscript Library and the literary collections of the Dodd Research Center, University of Connecticut, where Charles Olson's and some of Robert Creeley's materials reside.

Archived materials tell stories in fragmented, incomplete *sentences*. In a lecture, Susan Howe once referred to Gertrude Stein's 'perfect' definition of *sentence*: 'A sentence is partly.' So too our imaginative reconstructions of the past through the objects found in archives. Few poets have put archival work to such generative use as Howe. To me, she offers guidance where otherwise I may have become utterly lost in the wilderness of recorded thought. The brokenness of this song into poems, prose, found materials, and scattered correspondence traces remote emotions I bring, in brief acts of will, to present concern. I know no way but that which is given.

***

When Black Mountain student Fielding Dawson wrote that 'Black Mountain was freedom,' the creative freedom he celebrates remained a core principle through schisms, phases, and fractures, over twenty-three years of the college's existence. Yet actual freedom – regardless of race, politics, gender, or sexuality – was more elusive, and though Black Mountain created a progressive environment in which many of these insidious social barriers vanished, Buncombe County, North Carolina, was generally not as forgiving of trespass against society's prejudiced norms. Blacks in the South were not only denied equal rights and education, but were also stripped of their dignity and often subjected to humiliation and violence.

In 1944, ten years before *Brown v. Board of Education* and

the forced integration of schools and college campuses, the Black Mountain College community took steps to bring black students into their experiment. They faced condemnation from locals, the threat of attacks or closure, and a growing reputation as a haven for 'subversives' or 'communists,' but the college stood at the vanguard not just of fights for artistic and intellectual freedom, but also for a more explicit liberty: the inalienable rights that all citizens had been promised. At Black Mountain, arts practice and pedagogy sought to enact those liberties and extend those rights.

Faculty and student meetings were held regularly at BMC, and for the most part copious minutes were kept. The integration debate continued throughout almost the entire lifespan of the college, from the very beginnings with Rice to the early 1950s.

Like any institution in its position, elements within the faculty feared the repercussions of flouting Southern conventions. In a letter from theatre instructor Robert Wunsch to composer John Evarts dated April 3, 1944, we read,

> The drama seemed to come out of our differences of opinion on the question of admitting Negroes [. . .]. In one dramatic meeting after another we discussed whether or not we should take Negroes. Clark Foreman was of the opinion that the move was a wise one and called the people against such a move cowards and reactionaries. [. . .]
>
> We got to the edge of a decision that seemed satisfactory to most of the members of the faculty [. . .]. We set up immediately a community course on the texture of the South, the mind of the South, the temper of the South [. . .]. Instead of taking students now we allow an adult Negro, preferably a teacher, to come to one of the Institutes as a guest for several weeks this summer. [. . .] It is the better part of wisdom not to invite trouble by declaring open warfare against the South.

In fact, they did not take on a black member of faculty first, but decided to accept a young black student named Alma Stone, whose unpublished memoir of BMC is found in the State Archives. At twenty-three years old, Stone had a double major in English and Music from Spelman College, where she was valedictorian, and an MA in English from Atlanta University. She came to the music institute at Black Mountain to study piano. Here is how her memoir from 1995 begins:

> Black Mountain's leadership in the arts for the second half of the 20th century has been well documented [. . .]. Inadequately recognized is the fact that long before other southern schools integrated their campuses, Black Mountain College was enrolling black students. The University of N.C. at Chapel Hill opened its doors to Blacks in its graduate schools in 1951. Federal troops brought about forced integration at the University of Mississippi in 1962 [. . .] under considerable duress.
>
> By recruiting African American students as early as it did in 1944, Black Mountain College merited a first place position in the history of racial integration in the American South [. . .] It is time for this achievement to be acknowledged.

Her first impressions of the college are striking. Stone writes,

> No frills, no pretense awaited me at Black Mountain from its places and people. I felt at home, as much as any place I had ever been. [. . .]
> Mrs. Oliver Freud, daughter-in-law of Sigmund Freud, attended the art institute. Monica Mann, daughter of author Thomas Mann, was in the music program. We were told that Mrs. Freud had escaped

Nazi persecution by trudging over the Alps at night with a Swiss guide. Monica had witnessed the drowning of her young husband in a ship wreck as they sought refuge in America. Eventually I learned of others, both students and faculty members, who had fled Hitler's atrocities. The war was personalized in a new way as I saw these and other evidences of individual courage and sacrifice for themselves, their families, and the world of art.

Stone's fellow students saw her as an equal, and they learned important lessons together: 'At BMC, art was people,' she writes. 'My discomfort was part of my education to see and perceive!' But at the end of the summer, when she left the confines of the secluded campus for a bus station in town, she saw that the world outside – the intractable South – had not changed:

Black Mountain could manage to integrate persons of diverse races, classes, nationalities, and physical conditions in its community, but in Georgia, the state in which I was born, I was seen as one dimensional – Black – and therefore would be denied access to educational opportunities in its state institutions, opportunities I had demonstrated that I could use. This denial was not new to me. I should have known better than to think things had changed. The year was 1944. Though it wasn't easy for it to do so, Black Mountain College was ready for me; the rest of the white South, not yet.

In April 1947, the Freedom Riders stopped at Black Mountain and spent the night there. On June 20, 1947, Edward Lowinsky wrote in a letter, 'After a very positive experience of a few years with the interracial program our Faculty has decided to open admission to Black Mountain College to students of all races.' Also in 1947, black artists Jacob Lawrence and Gwendolyn

Knight came to the college, where Lawrence taught in the summer art institute. These advances led to a push for scholarships for black students, though local tensions remained high, and the progressive attitudes of the college continued to be tested. In a faculty meeting on November 21, 1951, Olson presented an ambivalent opinion:

> Mr Olson said that a student asked him if it was true that there is no discrimination at BM and that he said BM welcomes a student without any question of race, religion or politics but the fact that the average Negro in the south is confronted with such economic barriers would deter advising any to whom a recognized degree is important to enroll at BMC [. . .]

Almost ten years after its initial experiment with integration, Black Mountain College was still hesitant; Olson speaks in the language of placation, at once assuming openness and inclusion while implicitly upholding the prejudices of Southern segregation. In response, the composer and faculty member Lou Harrison stated flatly, 'there is a generality involved which is not true.'9

OFFICE MEMORANDUM   UNITED STATES
                                       GOVERNMENT

                                       DATE: 5/31/56

TO: DIRECTOR, FBI [J. Edgar Hoover]

FROM: SAC, CHARLOTTE (17-942)

SUBJECT: BLACK MOUNTAIN COLLEGE,
             Black Mountain, North Carolina
             VAM
             (OO: Charlotte)

On April 3, 1956, Mr. CECIL PATE, Chief Attorney, Veterans Administration Regional Office, Winston-Salem, N.C. arranged a conference between himself, Mr. JAMES DRUMMOND of the Vocational and Rehabilitation Division of the Veterans Administration, and SA CARMON J. STUART. Mr. PATE advised that his office was in the process of conducting a Compliance Inspection of the subject college and that he felt that the information which had been developed might involve a matter of internal security and that for this reason he desired SA STUART to sit in on the conference. Mr. DRUMMOND advised that a Summary of Compliance Survey Report was being compiled and that it would be submitted to Mr. PATE in the near future. Mr. DRUMMOND furnished no specific information indicating subversive or disloyal activity on the part of the students or instructors at the school.

Mr. PATE advised that when the Summary Report became available he would examine it with respect to possible fraud violations and if any were apparent he would refer this information to the Charlotte Division of the FBI.

On May 9, 1956, Mr. PATE made available a copy of the

Summary Compliance Survey Report, referred to above, and a memorandum synopsis of this Survey. Mr. PATE advised that on the basis of the information set out in the Survey Report he felt that the facts of this case should be discussed with the United States Attorney in Asheville, N.C., and that he would arrange for a conference with the United States Attorney and requested that an Agent be present at the conference. He stated that he would make all necessary records of his office available at the proposed conference.

The Summary Compliance Survey sets out information indicating that false statements regarding attendance of students at the subject college have been made by the college officials and that the veterans do not attend classes in the normal sense. The college has been certifying that certain veterans have been regularly attending but keeps no record of such attendance. Veteran Administration officials have taken steps which have resulted in the school's approval by the State Board of Education of North Carolina being withdrawn, thus cutting off subsistence of veterans. School officials have advised that they are conducting a very unusual type of school, for example, a student may do nothing all day and in the middle of the night may decide he wants to paint or write, which he does, and he may call upon his teachers at this time for guidance. They advised that everything is left to the desires of the individual. The Survey Report indicates that there are 23 students in the college, 9 of them are veterans.

This Office will open individual cases on each of the 9 students if the USA indicates that he contemplates prosecution and requests additional investigation.[10]

[Littleton, NH]
Thursday – Sept 28 [1950]

Dear O/

Okay, old friend, let's see yez cut this one to pieces. Fair enough. Hope it hits harder. Have thrown out much of the (red flags for me) related. Have tried to keep straight to the 'point' of what's under hand. Hope it comes so, for you.

[. . .]

Abt Black Mt. Ann says: right off. NO. Also, I don't even know what agronomy is. Perhaps, I misrepresent? I mean, we have here, small place, off on dirt road. I do things, chickens & like for sustenance. Not that I sell same, or much. The gig, that Ann has small amt of money, in trust, the income of which we can just make it on (and what else, what else), but, what it is, movement, even movies, not afforded. Easily or at all. But I wdn't give up same, the movement possible, even tho it's no beer (shit), etc., with this freedom. I like it fine, this way. And so, hating, loathing as I do, all educational clots, can't make or see thing with BMC. But yr thinking,

something else. Very grateful. Too often with me, I ask these things, & then when someone helps, like yrself, get almost bitter, that they sd get me out of it.

Well, Syracuse, let me hold out for that.

[. . .]

yr lad – Bob[11]

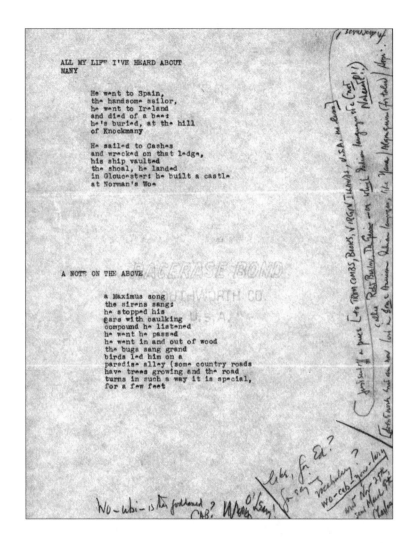

End of a letter from Charles Olson to Ed Dorn, March 1, 1958

Hunting through archives, you fall into ruin.

The dead here, they are weightless. They do

not know you've come, or why you search

in sundered objects, symbols of life you may

    represent again to another, exhibit an era.

    I hear your voices. I sit down beside your

    hands curling & turning, penned in margins,

    lines set to breaking free once your bones

        are battered away to chalk. These are for keeping.

        Those scribes cribbed divine notes on justice.

        We set a light by their crafting, songs for keeping.

        Just as, now blind, we walk through wild leaf, speaking.

In my mother's honours eleventh-grade American Literature class, we were made to memorize passages from Ralph Waldo Emerson:

*'The great man is he who in the midst of the crowd keeps with perfect sweetness the independence of solitude.'***

For many years I carried that line around with me. I still often carry a handsome, leather-bound, pocket-sized edition of Emerson's essays. More recently I was drawn to his 'On Experience':

'The only thing grief has taught me is to know how shallow it is.'

With numb sorrow and futile regret, clarity breaks through where once age obscured thought from the mind. Directly, for once, we speak.

** 'What I must do is all that concerns me, and not what the people think. This rule, equally as arduous in actual and in intellectual life, may serve for the whole distinction between greatness and meanness. It is the harder, because you will always find those who think they know what is your duty better than you know it. It is easy in the world to live after the world's opinion; it is easy in solitude to live after your own; but the great man is he who in the midst of the crowd keeps with perfect sweetness the independence of solitude.' ('Self-Reliance' – Ralph Waldo Emerson)

I have trespassed into the disciplines of American Studies and Textual Criticism through my need to fathom what wildness and absolute freedom is the nature of expression. There are other characteristic North American voices and visions that remain antinomian and separatist. In order to hear them I have returned by strange paths to a particular place at a particular time, a threshold at the austere reach of the book [. . .].

I am drawn toward the disciplines of history and literary criticism but in the dawning distance a dark wall of rule supports the structure of every letter, record, transcript: every proof of authority and power. I know records are compiled by winners, and scholarship is in collusion with Civil Government. I know this and go on searching for some trace of love's infolding through all the paper in all the libraries I come to.

Susan Howe, *The Birth-Mark* (1993)

New England Sound

for Susan Howe

In your time
I sense the latter

Circumference –
we know now

to which it
refers, outward / &

inward, at once.

You make a certain
understanding

stand for letters
we read under

light of a desk lamp,
lingering

soft light
the petals

of red flowers
the words

are homophones –
our desire

fades quickly,
underneath

Berlin

[architecture]

I hunt among stones

Charles Olson

I made of the City
an incommunicate song –

Danced – joy to wonder –
infallible nightsteps

through a palace of stone.
Wide avenues below me

told stories. Words I taught
fell still – ached alone in invisible

forms no History enveloped,
left information cold, unwanted – unused.

I made of love
an inconsummate dream –

Breathed – so Heaven wandered –
and in that movement

gathered views beyond
no word could tell, nor city hold,

nor love remember.

The Architect, by his arrangement of forms, realizes an order which is a pure creation of his spirit; by forms and shapes he affects our senses to an acute degree and provokes plastic emotions; by the relationships which he creates he wakes profound echoes in us, he gives us the measure of an order which we feel to be in accordance with that of our world, he determines the various movements of our heart and of our understanding; it is then that we experience the sense of beauty.

Le Corbusier, *Toward a New Architecture* (1931)

I arrived in Berlin mid-winter. On a government grant, for three months I intended to uncover Black Mountain in the *Bauhaus-Archiv*.

A city of wide avenues and stone met me. The architecture of the twentieth century seemed, for the first time, something (somehow) apparent. This was not a city of dreams. Rather, a city of so many pasts that all sat somewhere near the surface. Scratching lightly, layer upon layer is revealed.

***

There would have been no Black Mountain – as it was – without the Bauhaus.

In 1919, Bauhaus founder Walter Gropius published a manifesto. The text sat opposite the famous woodcut *Cathedral* by Lyonel Feininger.

> The ultimate goal of all art is the building! The ornamentation of the building was once the main purpose of the visual arts, and they were considered indispensable parts of the great building. Today, they exist in complacent isolation, from which they can only be salvaged by the purposeful and cooperative endeavours of all artisans. Architects, painters and sculptors must learn a new way of seeing and understanding the composite character of the building, both as a totality and in terms of its parts. Their work will then re-imbue itself with the spirit of architecture, which it lost in salon art.
>
> The art schools of old were incapable of producing this unity – and how could they, for art may not be taught. They must return to the workshop. This world of mere drawing and painting of draughtsmen and applied artists must at long last become a world

that builds. When a young person who senses within himself a love for creative endeavour begins his career, as in the past, by learning a trade, the unproductive 'artist' will no longer be condemned to the imperfect practice of art because his skill is now preserved in craftsmanship, where he may achieve excellence.

Architects, sculptors, painters – we all must return to craftsmanship! For there is no such thing as 'art by profession.' There is no essential difference between the artist and the artisan. The artist is an exalted artisan. Merciful heaven, in rare moments of illumination beyond man's will, may allow art to blossom from the work of his hand, but the foundations of proficiency are indispensable to every artist. This is the original source of creative design.

Black Mountain was a built world designed for democracy. Study in craft and design. The poem as craft and design. Apprentice; journeyman; master. New ways in a New World. *There is no such thing as art by profession.*

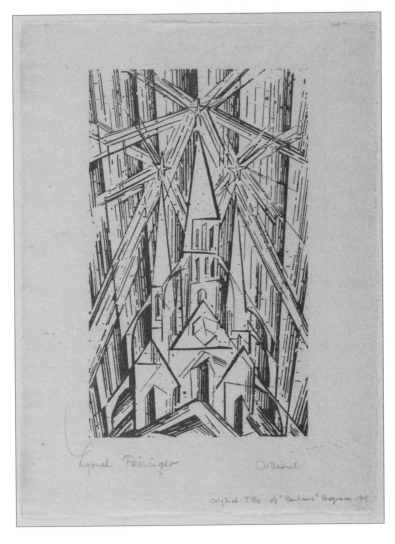

Cathedral, by Lionel Feininger, 1919[12]
Courtesy of the Museum of Modern Art

In 1919, Walter Gropius united the Grand Ducal Saxon Academy of Fine Arts and the Grand Ducal Saxon School of Arts and Crafts in Weimar. With this visionary act modelled on the medieval craft guilds, he intended to unify the so-called 'fine' arts with crafts. The artistic ideal was the building, province of the exulted Architect. His political statement was the vision of a new world – one in which the arts exist for a common purpose, with the building as its final manifestation. By reaffirming the centrality of craft to all arts, the aim was to produce a new kind of professional. Artists' designs were to be commonplace in common homes. The world made simple, beautiful, and functional. Both political and artistic *ECONOMY*.

A hero of the First World War, Gropius was a charismatic and dashing man. When he founded the Bauhaus, he was also the husband of Alma Mahler, whose notoriety added to Gropius's lustre. Few knew just how fraught their marriage was, though many had their suspicions and spread society gossip. Nevertheless, Gropius let nothing deter him from his singular focus on the Bauhaus. In time, even Alma's other lovers – including the poet Franz Werfel – became supporters of the institution.

The Bauhaus mirrored the life of the Weimar Republic, the most liberal constitution in Europe after the First World War.

The new government seated in Weimar established its constitution in the central city of German Enlightenment, with all the associations and connotations that came with it: the city of Goethe, Bach, Luther, Schiller, and Liszt. The Republic's fourteen-year life matches that of the Bauhaus, from 1919 to 1933.

Like the short-lived push for representative democracy in the German interwar period, the Bauhaus died with the rise of National Socialism.

Glass & Steel. *Blood & Soil.*

Integration of *Art* & *Life.*

Bauhaus pedagogy demanded a return to fundamentals.

This meant a study of the elements of form. And Gropius believed that new forms of artistic practice and organisation would lead to similar transformations in society.

New ways of seeing give us visions of a new world. It is up to us to design and build it.

Bauhaus student, and later master, Josef Albers believed,

Through works of art we are permanently reminded to be balanced within ourselves and with others; to have respect for proportions; that is, to keep relationships. It teaches us to be disciplined, and selective between quantity and quality. Art teaches the educational world that it is too little to collect only knowledge; furthermore, that economy is not a matter of statistics, but of a sufficient proportion between effort and effect.

Art problems are problems of human relationship. Note that balance, proportion, harmony, coordination are tasks of our daily life, as are also activity, intensity, economy, and unity. And learn that behavior results in form – and, reciprocally, form influences behavior.[13]

Naturally, man's relation to his fellows is not so easily perfected. Like Black Mountain, the Bauhaus was plagued by internal battles and, at times, all-out civil war.

Appointed in 1919, painter Johannes Itten developed the Bauhaus course in first-year fundamentals, known as the *Vorkurs*. According to Magdalena Droste, Itten's teaching principle 'can be summarized in a pair of opposites':

> 'intuition and method,' or 'subjective experience and objective recognition' [. . .]. The discovery of rhythm and the harmonious composition of different rhythms were among the recurring themes of his classes, which were divided into three main areas: studies of natural objects and materials, the analysis of Old Masters and life drawing.[14]

Itten's basic course was to be the foundation for all students entering Bauhaus workshops and central to their new ways of seeing and perceiving the world. The school attempted to strike balance between art and industry, craft and design, theory and applied techniques. *Rhythm* and *Harmony*.

Before coming to the Bauhaus, Itten had run his own art school in Vienna. His teaching and his paintings were, for the most part, highly regarded. But it was his eccentric personality – not his teaching of form and materials – that attracted most attention in Weimar. Itten's *Vorkurs* was centred on intuitive perception found through meditation. He emphasized the personality and individuality of the artist, while his own mystical personality put him at odds with Gropius's vision for the school. Itten's followers copied his shaven head, monastic robes, and extreme diet, the antithesis of Gropius's meticulously modern, dapper appearance. Their approaches to art and teaching widely diverged. Gropius argued for more discipline from students and less hero worship, less *self-expression*. He wanted the *Vorkurs* and the Bauhaus as a whole to prepare students for the economies of the future, not to guide them into mystical cults. Gropius's hold on power at the Bauhaus was more or less absolute, and he forced Itten's resignation in 1922. As was the case at Black Mountain, conflicts at the Bauhaus were often initiated by one powerful figure with strong convictions. Sooner or later, house clearing became necessary to keep balance.

In 1923, after Itten's departure, Gropius hired the Hungarian painter and photographer, László Moholy-Nagy to take over the fundamentals course. He modified Itten's metaphysical approach with one centred on the machine. Decidedly Constructivist, Moholy-Nagy was interested in the mechanisation of the modern world, and he believed that the arts must utilize new technologies. His thinking was in line with Gropius's push for greater interaction between the arts and industry.

While the Bauhaus offered new hope for arts education, conditions in contemporary German society continued to deteriorate. Politics in Weimar shifted the ground beneath the Bauhaus, which was dependent on city funding. Though it was not affiliated with one political party or another, the school naturally attracted those with radical ideas. They were routinely labelled Bolshevists, and Gropius was called on again and again to defend the school in public and in print. Under the political strain, Weimar could no longer support the Bauhaus. Many members of the community, including Albers, questioned the school's continued existence, but Gropius forged ahead. Several cities came forward to court the school, and in the end the industrial city of Dessau was chosen, while the ascendance of political factions on both the far right and far left in Germany continued to threaten the school's existence.

In Dessau, far from illustrious Weimar, Gropius created the emblematic Bauhaus. He designed the building himself, and with it the physical manifestation of his educational and artistic ideals. The glass-steel-and-concrete building housed all of the disciplines and workshops under one roof. The design laid bare the building's functions. The walls were unadorned. Stairs and hallways were made so that apprentices and masters would encounter one another regularly; the school and its physical plant served a social function. Through active participation in this kind of community, the restoration of Germany might live up to the ideals of the Weimar Republic. While contemporary politics threatened such utopian ideas, Gropius maintained faith in an approach to learning and practising art that would lead to the transformation of society.

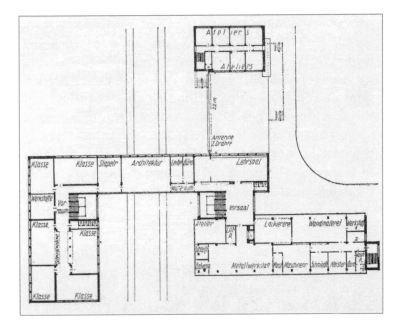

Gropius Design for the Bauhaus, Dessau
Courtesy of Bauhaus-Archiv / Museum für Gestaltung, Berlin

The move to Dessau in 1925 meant increased possibility in matching design with industry. Though Moholy-Nagy remained nominal head of the *Vorkurs*, Josef Albers was handling most of the teaching. He had come to the Bauhaus to focus on his work as an artist and to get away from his elementary teaching career. The constant power struggles within the Bauhaus and the heavy teaching schedule made him consider departure for Berlin.

In 1925, Albers married Anneliese Fleischmann, a student at the Bauhaus rebelling against her parents' expectations. Anni came from a wealthy Jewish family in Berlin who were powerful in the publishing industry. She was strong-willed and had a conviction for the arts that matched her husband's. Yet even at the Bauhaus, where women at times made up a large part of the community, their roles were circumscribed. They could not study the 'higher' arts of architecture and painting, but the 'crafts' were left open to them. Anni entered the weaving workshop. Her work in that medium opened up entirely new possibilities for the form.

Perhaps inevitably, word spread in Dessau that the Bauhaus was a hotbed of radicalism. Indeed, the politics of some students caused significant problems. Many aligned themselves with the Communist cause, and as Dessau came under greater influence of the Nazi party, the city became increasingly wary of the Bauhaus association. Gropius expelled the Communist students and tried once again to root the school in its fundamental purposes. Could his vision of a new world built with new forms not transcend the old realities?

In 1928, there was a mass exodus of influential figures from the Bauhaus, which included the resignations of key figures Marcel Breuer, Herbert Bayer, Moholy-Nagy, and eventually Walter Gropius himself. The same year, Swiss architect Hannes Meyer took over as director of the Bauhaus, but he was not able to exert any more control over the political tide threatening to overwhelm the school. Meyer also disagreed with Albers's approach to the *Vorkurs*, thinking it too experimental and theoretical when the students should be concerned with more practical, social matters. (He failed to see the social revolution inherent in Albers's experimental approach.)

In 1927, Meyer had been tasked with setting up the first official architecture department at the school, this having been a glaring omission for an institution run by Walter Gropius and founded on the principle of the building as the highest form of functional art. (During Gropius's time, 'Bauhaus' architectural projects were run out of his Berlin office.) Meyer's architecture was marked by his leftist, socialist leanings. He supported students who protested against the *Vorkurs* and in favour of a doctrinaire Communist agenda. In 1930, Meyer was dismissed as director by the Dessau city government, an indication that the rift between far-right and far-left factions in Germany was becoming more pronounced and hazardous.

Architect Ludwig Mies van der Rohe was appointed Bauhaus director in 1930, and he attempted to banish politics from the school while maintaining the focus on architecture and the building. Despite efforts by Mies and the rest of the community, the Dessau city government, under political pressure, defunded the Bauhaus in 1932. With limited financial means, Mies managed to move the school to Berlin briefly. Classes began there in January of 1933, the same month Adolf Hitler became chancellor of Germany. Nazis hounded the school and its director, declaring the Bauhaus a Bolshevist haven, planting evidence of leftist political activity, and eventually mandating the closure of the school.

By that time, the Bauhaus had become Mies van der Rohe's private school, with its original purpose much diminished. Yet Albers continued teaching up to the very end. After only fourteen years, the Bauhaus was shut. Founded by Gropius as a visionary experiment intent on changing Germany for the better, the school had supported some of the most revolutionary artists of the period: Gropius, Albers, Paul Klee, Wassily Kandinsky, Bayer, Breuer, Xanti Schawinsky, and so many others. Yet it suffered the same calamity that forced many of those artists to flee Europe.

Assault on the Bauhaus 1932, by Iwao Yamawaki[15]
Courtesy of the Yamawaki Iwao & Michiko Archives

In 1937, Moholy-Nagy became director of the New Bauhaus in Chicago. Mies van der Rohe settled in the US, teaching at the Armour Institute. Also in 1937, Lyonel Feininger moved to New York City, where he had been born. His works in Germany were destroyed by the Nazis, and it took some time for his reputation to grow in the US. Finally, in 1944, he was given a retrospective in the New York Museum of Modern Art. In 1945, twenty-six years after his *Cathedral* illustrated the Bauhaus manifesto, Feininger taught at the summer institute at Black Mountain. Xanti Schawinsky, a brilliant painter and designer who developed groundbreaking forms of experimental theatre at the Bauhaus, came to Black Mountain in 1936 and developed his concept of Spectodrama, an important forerunner to the multidisciplinary performance art of later decades.

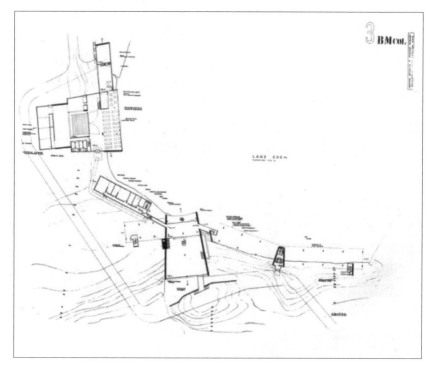

The Gropius-Breuer Plan for BMC, Black Mountain Bulletin
Courtesy of the Western Regional Archives, State Archives of North Carolina

Gropius landed at Harvard, where he became a professor of architecture in the Graduate School of Design. In 1949, he designed the Graduate Center of Harvard University. Gropius became an important part of Black Mountain's story (and its architecture) when in 1939 he and Breuer were asked to design a complex of buildings on the college's new grounds at Lake Eden. Though their plans were never constructed for lack of financing, it is clear that Gropius's vision for Black Mountain was similar to his Dessau building.

The Studies Building under construction
Courtesy of the Western Regional Archives, State Archives of North Carolina

The design includes communal, interactive spaces consonant with Bauhaus and Black Mountain educational ideals. It would have housed individual studies, workshops, music rooms, living spaces, and a multipurpose dining hall and theatre. When initial fundraising efforts were unsuccessful, and the entry of the US into the European war was imminent, the community at Black

Mountain had to abandon the ambitious Gropius-Breuer proposal. Instead, in 1940, the college hired Lawrence Kocher, an American architect with ideas sympathetic to the Bauhaus and modern architecture, to design a scaled-back version. Kocher planned the Studies Building on Lake Eden, and the structure was built by Black Mountain students and faculty.

The Studies Building
Courtesy of the Western Regional Archives, State Archives of North Carolina

In 1964, Gropius presented architectural plans for a Bauhaus archive in Darmstadt. Echoing so many turns in these intertwined stories, politics and financial realities dashed the idea, but eventually the *Bauhaus-Archiv*, designed by Gropius and modified by his colleague Alex Cvijanovic, was built in West Berlin in 1979. I arrived there in 2015.

The Bauhaus Archive

Courtesy of Bauhaus-Archiv / Museum für Gestaltung, Berlin

In research libraries and collections, we may capture
the portrait of history in so-called insignificant visual
and verbal textualities and textiles. In material details.
In twill fabrics, bead-work pieces, pricked patterns,
four-ringed knots, tiny spangles, sharp-toothed sten-
cil wheels; in quotations, thought-fragments, rhymes,
syllables, anagrams, graphemes, endangered phonemes,
in soils and cross-outs.

– Susan Howe, *Spontaneous Particulars* (2014)

Decades after re-unification, the radical approach and practices of the Bauhaus have been thoroughly integrated into our
contemporary visual world. Yet when I approach the buildings
across the Landwehrkanal in Tiergarten, I am struck by simple,

repeated curves, concrete and glass. White and gray midwinter light reflects off the rounded surfaces and flat planes. The fundamental elements of architecture and design, articulated intelligently: the repository for the Bauhaus's material legacy.

we may capture the portrait of history

***

Giving up the Horse . . .

Theodore ('Ted') Dreier was – in many ways – the unsung hero of Black Mountain College. John Andrew Rice receives much of the credit for the college's founding, though Dreier was at his side following the famous 'Rollins fracas' and remained a central member of the college community for the first sixteen years of its existence. Dreier was never the outspoken and confrontational pedagogue that Rice was. Yet his contributions to the college were just as, if not more, important to its survival than anyone else's. Through his dogged commitment, patient accounting, and relentless fundraising, Black Mountain College continued operation through immense difficulty. Dreier gave much of his life to the college, which could never have survived without him.

Ted Dreier at Black Mountain
Helen Post Modley Collection
Western Regional Archives, State Archives of North Carolina

An engineer with a degree from Harvard, Dreier always wished he could spend more time teaching at Black Mountain. He was listed in various Black Mountain Bulletins as the instructor in mathematics and physics. Later, he spent a great deal of time preparing a course on the 'Philosophy of Science.' Yet most of the time, he found himself in charge (first as treasurer, later as rector) of the college's finances and its physical plant. Many of his wealthy contacts were called upon time and time again to rescue Black Mountain from collapse. Dreier had an unshakable belief in the college's mission, so eloquently put forward by Rice from the beginning, but he matched that ideological commitment with a practical ability to raise funds and attract supporters – the much-needed 'Friends of the College.' His family lived at Black Mountain, and his son – Ted Jr. – grew up and studied there. The distressing chapter of Dreier's Black Mountain story came years after Rice's departure, when – after the Second World War – the college went through its most difficult and trying period.

As an American of German descent, Dreier had very close relationships with Walter and Ise Gropius, as well as their daughter Ati, who graduated from Black Mountain College in 1946 and was godmother to the Dreiers' daughter. As founder of the Bauhaus, Gropius had great influence over Black Mountain. Though he never served there on a permanent basis, he was a member of the Board of Advisors, taught at the famous summer art institutes, and acted in generous friendship toward Black Mountain and the Dreier family. Having influential friends like Gropius remained necessary for Black Mountain's survival.

In the *Bauhaus-Archiv*, a portion of Gropius's collected correspondence illustrates the close relationship his family had with the Dreiers. It also tells the story of Ted Dreier's disillusionment and, finally, his departure from the radical institution he played such a large part in creating.

One letter to Dreier shows the sacrifices Gropius was willing to make in order to allow his daughter Ati to continue her education at Black Mountain:

> I had meant to write to you regarding Ati when your letter arrived. Meanwhile I have carefully checked up on my financial status regarding a second college year for Ati. I have given up my horse, our second car and we put up a roomer in Ati's room. After this the utmost my shrunken budget allows me to spend for Ati's next college year is 1000$. I should like to leave it to you to decide which may be the better way for Ati to make good on the difference either in your summer camp or here in war work. [16]

In response, Dreier assured Gropius that Ati might find work as part of the summer music institute – work that would not be so demanding as in a war factory or on the college farm, and which would allow her time and energy to pursue her studies in art. On April 26, Dreier wrote, 'Ati was quite jealous of my having heard from you before she did but she was really extremely happy to think that there was a good chance now of her coming back next year [. . .]. I have a feeling myself that it would be a good thing and I believe that the Albers agree with me.'

Many other letters between Dreier and Gropius sketch a close, familial relationship. They invite one another and their families for visits to Cambridge, Black Mountain, and New York; they recount holidays together and hopes for putting the college's affairs in order. Dreier even wrote to Ise Gropius about the possibility of moving to Germany after the war:

> The other day we had a faculty candidate for history who had been in Military Government in Germany for a year speak. He had been Educational and Fine Arts Officer [. . .]. Most people liked his talk which was certainly very interesting, but there is something that bothers me terribly about the kind of aloof objectivity with which such a man can talk about Germany and the people and the problems of education and denazification.
>
> Although I am naturally not considering any such thing seriously because I still hope things may work out here at Black Mountain (and please consider my mentioning it confidential), the idea had crossed my mind that if I left maybe a place that I could be of as much use as any would be in Germany [. . .]. But the very thought of living comfortably in a country while everyone else was half-starving and discouraged is something that would be almost impossible to do if one has any feelings for the people at all.

Dreier included Gropius in the mailing of his resignation from Black Mountain. On August 31, 1948, Dreier wrote to Walter and Ise: 'This is just a line to say that the die is finally cast. A few days ago I came to the conclusion that I simply could not undertake another reorganization of the college [. . .]. I said I wanted to leave.' In fact, Dreier stayed on just a bit longer in order to help transition to the leadership of Josef Albers as college rector.

Beside personal correspondence, one of the most fascinating pieces in the Gropius collection is Ted Dreier's 'Summary Report – Black Mountain College: the First 15 ½ Years,' written as part of his forced resignation.[17] The ten-page document was written at a point when Dreier was understandably frustrated and bitter, yet the clarity (and even charity) of his writing still comes through when addressing the core principles of the Black Mountain experiment. He writes, 'For 15 ½ years Black Mountain has stood for a non-political radicalism in higher education which, like all true radicalism, sought to find modern means for getting back to fundamentals.' This, he concedes, was largely achieved in the early years, and the character of the college under Albers exemplified these ideals. Dreier saw the reconstitution of the college after the war as the period in which things changed. Infighting was rampant. Younger members of staff who – Dreier points out – had no connection to the foundation of the college advocated divergent pedagogies. 'There has to be agreement,' Dreier wrote, 'about method as well as about aim, and readiness to follow the method.'

Yet Dreier had not entirely given up hope for Black Mountain, even as he knew his time there was finished: 'If the effort is made to continue the College it will have to be made by others who may or may not stand for what Black Mountain has stood for in the past.' Even in despair, Dreier anticipated a rebirth of the college. This is exactly what would happen, very much in the way Dreier describes. When Charles Olson became the dominant force at Black Mountain in the early 1950s, he looked back to the founding principles laid out by Rice and Dreier, while also looking toward a future that would be, in many ways, quite different. Olson's Black Mountain – and especially his style of leadership – would probably not have elicited Dreier's enthusiasm.

(We must recognize that Olson's leadership finally failed; he was not the organizer and fundraiser that Dreier had been.) In the end, it was Olson – not Dreier – who had to spend years liquidating the college's assets and setting its affairs in order. But after Dreier's departure, the college did gain new life. Many people today know of Black Mountain through the Olson phase, which included writers Robert Creeley and Robert Duncan, and the creation *of The Black Mountain Review*. (These writers set up their own, informal poetic *Vorkurs* during the college's final stages – a return to poetic fundamentals.) However, Dreier must be given his due. If it weren't for his consistent efforts on behalf of the institution, there would have been no place at Lake Eden for those who followed.

In 1933, two other Bauhaus refugees fled to the United States. When Josef and Anni Albers arrived at Black Mountain College, Josef was asked what he planned to teach. In his limited English, he famously replied: 'to open eyes.'

Albers writes, '[M]ore important than to have a culture . . . [is] that the people here [in the US] are very hungry for a culture.'[18] Later it would be argued, 'for the artists who taught there, Black Mountain was a sojourn of great fertility, and like the shaman who travels in quest of experience, these artists derived significant personal strength from their artistic voyages.'[19] Yet the Alberses made a home at Black Mountain for fourteen years. For the German couple, the college became the centre of their extraordinary creative lives, while providing an American context for their groundbreaking pedagogy.

In his introduction to a book on Albers, *To Open Eyes*, Frederick A. Horowitz (a former student of the master) writes, 'Albers was a revolutionary whose ideas and practices liberated art training from the academy and shaped it into something fresh and forward looking.' Through his early teaching experiences in Germany, Albers learned that 'successful teaching does not depend on small classes' and that 'large classes have the advantage of mutual learning from and with each other.'[20] He would find that Black Mountain, with its communal living and shared responsibility for basic survival, was one large classroom with virtually no boundaries, where students were largely responsible for their own education.

Josef and Anni Albers at Black Mountain College
Courtesy of the Western Regional Archives, State Archives of North Carolina

The war and the fall of the Weimar Republic initiated Albers into fraught political realities. As the century marched on and atrocities mounted, the Alberses were forced to watch from overseas. Horowitz tells us that in Albers's Germany, 'as is frequently the case, goals for education were rooted in political imperatives. After Prussia's victory over France in the Franco-Prussian war in 1870 and the unification of Germany [. . .] educational reform became linked to the largely economic goals of Germany's postwar reconstruction.'[21] The formation of education and culture are inherently political manifestations; this was not lost on Black Mountain, where even in an Eden isolated from the world, politics shaped what unfolded.

In a real sense, Albers united the struggles of Europe and the United States, and the instigations of the Bauhaus and Black Mountain. His pragmatism also fit into the Dewey-Rice ethos. As Horowitz writes, Albers, 'decried both "undisciplined laissez-faire" and "imitative parroting" as strategies for art education, saying that "shooting without aim" was as senseless as "shooting at objects already shot."'[22] Albers understood, as Dewey did, that the educator 'like the artist [. . .] has the problem of creating something that is not the exact duplicate of anything that has been wrought and achieved previously.'[23] Black Mountain opened up a field of activity wherein disciplinary poles, the new and the old, the tried and the experimental, would interact.

Albers was the embodiment of these interactions. His approach and pedagogy quickly emerged as the high standard at Black Mountain, as it left room for each individual's approach while demanding a 'mastery of [art] materials or means, achieved over a lifetime.' He carried on the Bauhaus basics at Black Mountain, training all students (not just those intent on becoming professional artists) in the fundamentals of colour, materials, perspective, and design. These were not skills gained merely for personal expression, just as the education at Black Mountain was not meant for personal distinction, but for use and function. Harris writes,

The curriculum that Albers developed at Black Mountain offered an alternative to both academic tradition and self-expression. Its content was a study of the elements of form; its method one of discovery and invention; its goal 'a constant and accurate "seeing and perceiving."' He noted that 'in art, as in all communication, precision – as to the effect wanted – and discipline – as to means used – are decisive.' Both can be achieved through experience, through continuous and repeated experimentation.[24]

Albers also fit into the overall character of the college as an experiment in intentional living:

Collective, agrarian democracies [Albers perceived] as 'social art' which 'become an equivalent to the seizure of the means of production since it refused sovereignty to material possessions and thereby denied their ability to dominate social relations.'[25]

Such egalitarian attitudes would reverberate in Albers's later teaching. His attitude to material possessions is contained in the aphorism from *Poems and Drawings*, 'To distribute material possessions / is to divide them / to distribute spiritual possessions / is to multiply them.'

This points to the Eastern influence so prevalent at Black Mountain, in the thinking of John Cage for instance, or the famous summer institute that included two of Japan's great craftsmen, Shōji Hamada and Sōetsu Yanagi, or the suffocating, indomitable Kudzu vine that spread over the mountain, a potent symbol. When Henry Miller visited Black Mountain, he noted, 'from the steps of BMC in North Carolina one has a view of mountains and forests which makes one dream of Asia.'[26]

Albers's pedagogy had a direct influence on many other

teachers and artists who came through Black Mountain, both in the normal school year and during the summer institutes. Even the so-called Black Mountain poets were aware of Albers's teaching. Robert Duncan said of his own classes at the college,

> I just had what would be anybody's idea of what Albers must have been doing. You knew that [Albers's students] had color theory, and that they did a workshop sort of approach, and that they didn't aim at a finished painting . . . I thought 'Well, that's absolutely right' . . . I think we had five weeks of vowels . . . and syllables . . . Numbers enter into poetry as they do in all time things, measurements. But . . . [with] Albers . . . it's not only the color, but it's the interrelationships of space and numbers.[27]

In his role as interim rector after Rice, Albers invited Olson to BMC for the first time, and the American poet recognized the strength of Albers's approach. In a letter from Black Mountain, dated August 7, 1951, Olson writes to W. H. ('Ping') Ferry,

> American education [must] move out into a more alive approach to its job [. . .] so that education as knowledge alone (as 'history') be *interlocked* with the arts and the sciences, interlock itself with the active work active men & women are doing.[28]

Duberman points out that 'in the process of working with paints, sounds and words, Rice thought the student might very well express something of his inner being, but in his view, the far more important educative aspects of the 'art-experience' lay elsewhere – in the discovery of 'integrity' [. . .]. That was the integrity of the artist. That should be the integrity of man as man.'[29] It is no wonder that Rice saw such promise in Albers in 1933. When Duberman interviewed Albers in 1967, he noted

that the German is 'distrustful of words – especially when ana-
lytical and in English – and so mindful of his integrity that he
constantly makes you feel threatened in your own.'[30] Albers's
insistence to Duberman, which echoes Fielding Dawson's line,
I find most useful:

> When it comes to an educational institution like Black
> Mountain [. . .] where teaching was to some extent
> the most important concern [. . .] let's not tell fact for
> fact in order to have it done once more; as we can-
> not repeat the Bauhaus, so we cannot repeat Black
> Mountain College [. . .] [We must] produce *actual*
> facts. That's my terminology. It means giving state-
> ments and formulations which lead further [. . .]. And
> so if you get for yourself some experience of a new
> insight, by discussing this institution . . . if there is an
> essence that was for you providing new experience [. . .]
> that is helping you to develop yourself further . . . this
> work on Black Mountain must directly or indirectly
> state some growth in your mind and in your looking
> at education.[31]

Examining the social and political significance of Black
Mountain illuminates the struggles of our own day. We still
need Black Mountain, though it cannot be exactly replicated.
Through archives, exposition, arrangement, and creation, I am
here to access *actual facts*, understanding, at the moment of contact, the objects of this development, through the poem, through
prose, to build new forms. Both Josef and Anni Albers were great
artists, writers, and teachers. We may return to their work again
and again to find fresh examples of how to live a noble life, and
also how to design our systems of education so that we get to
the core of their purpose. Olson recognized Albers's impact on
these developments:

Why I like Albers is, that, right then & there he was
flexible [. . .]. And so it happened, that, as I found out
from Robert Payne, later, between Albers and myself
a method of education which has long been the law
of Chinese education got applied again, here: that is,
that a so-called creative man stays at his own last in
a capital city [for Olson, Washington, D.C., and the
Roosevelt Administration], doing his work where men
ought to do their work, in the midst of active society
[. . .] where, as I say, work can be accomplished [. . .].
But that fact shouldn't, any longer, deprive education
of what it so very much needs – the active professional
man, in the arts and in the fields of knowledge, who is
not an historian (as, basically, all 'professors' are) but
is himself a maker of 'history', eh?[32]

Artists, teachers, and students at Black Mountain made history. Echoes of the Bauhaus are inescapable. As communal as
both institutions aimed to be, it was the creative individual who
remained the source of power and movement.

Built worlds of form and function. An architectural prose – and
scaffold of poetry.

find modern means for getting back to fundamentals . . .

Josef Albers teaching at Black Mountain
Courtesy of the Western Regional Archives, State Archives of North Carolina

Josef Albers

Speech given at the general meeting of Bl. Mnt. Coll. in the beginning of the year Sept. 12 1939. [From the Gropius Papers, *Bauhaus-Archiv*][33]

Black Mountain College
is starting a new year with more new students
than ever before
and with bigger and larger plans than ever before –
while Europe – traditionally our cultural background –
is starting war.
A war of which I can't see any end –
until a certain *Weltanschauung*
based on power through organisation
is overthrown,
until the ideology based on the belief
that one man can decide the fate of millions of people –
is destroyed.
In this situation – where followers – or masses – that is uncreative
   crew –

make such forces possible,
it seems to me necessary to emphasize
that the ultimate aim of education is – humanity.

Humanity I understand here as a balance
    between dependence and independence –
    the two divergent directions
    in which education is engaged.

But balance is a problem of proportion.
Usually proportion is understood as an art term.
It means that different activities keep a certain order
in which every element is related to all the other elements.

When art essentially is documentation of life.
Then we should learn from the arts
that proportion is a very important problem of living.

Here we are right in the middle of one of our beliefs.
Our belief in Community life.
It is an old habit of beliefs to formulate phrases
but is good to think over phrases.

Let me pick out one B. M. C. phrase concerning our community
        idea:
                'Group influence'.
We know there is no group thinking and no group feeling
                as there are no creative masses.
Consequently there is no real group influence.

Real influence is personal radiation
and doing something is educationally
                far more than talking about something –
                as philosophy is more than dialectics.
Nobody has the right to expect something from others
that he is not able or willing to do himself.
In order to say that positively, I have to repeat the
old saying: The example is the strongest educational means.

If we all are aware of this old wisdom
then we will realize that the most important thing
in education is self-education.
That cultivating a group means growth of the individual
that growth does not come out of pulling and pushing
but needs sun and rain – and that criticism
has to help.

If we concentrate on self-education that is
on changing ourselves before changing others

then the separation between those only serving
and those only being served will disappear,
which means social improvement.
Then we will break through the boundary between
those teaching and those being taught.
>   Because then everybody will be educator and
>   student at the same time.
At the same time – I believe – that concentration on
ourself and our work will make us estimate again as more
>   competent
those experiences and more insight.

If I may connect again our situation here and the infernal fight
>   abroad.
I like to believe that in this fight
between strength and power
or between quality and quantity
B. M. C. is consciously on the side of Laotse who says:
He is the leader who does not want to lead.
And with the Mayan Indians
who demanded that the King be the most cultivated among
>   them.

Anni Albers weaving
Courtesy of the Western Regional Archives, State Archives of North Carolina

The difficult problems are the fundamental problems;
simplicity stands at the end, not at the beginning of a
work. If education can lead us to elementary seeing,
away from too much and too complex information,
to the quietness of vision and discipline of forming, it
again may prepare us for the task ahead, working for
today and tomorrow.

– Anni Albers, BMC, March 7, 1941

When art essentially is documentation of life.
Then we should learn from the arts
that proportion is a very important problem of living.
The example is the strongest educational means.

Josef Albers in the Garden Teaching, by Ruth O'Neil
Courtesy of the Western Regional Archives, State Archives of North Carolina

I want to congratulate you upon the work you are doing. You are here as a little community to work with your hands and your brains, which is a good thing for you. What is done out of pleasure is much better done than what is done out of duty. If you had to climb mountains out of duty, you could not mount these high mountains. I think that is also true with the high mountains of the spirit.

– Albert Einstein on Black Mountain College

my 2 years at black mountain college, n.c.   ,   with an introduction.

xanti schawinsky

in 1933 i had fled from berlin to switzerland, and later set-tled in rapallo in italy to paint. the following two years i spent in milan, where i had been commissioned with design jobs by motta, olivetti, italian line, the review 'natura', illy of trieste, bruzzichelli of florence, the corso theatre of zurich, san pellegrino, globestar of paris, pyroil and champion – to mention a few, and i joined the young group of italian abstract painters around the galleria del milione where my work also was exhibited. these friends repeatedly expressed to me their liberal views which they regarded as nonconforming with italian fascism which had cut off the spiritual and artistic life of their country from the rest of the world. it was them who had invited me to come to milan, after i was introduced to them by the architect luciano baldessari, a pioneer and a friend of mine. i wrote to paul klee, w. kandinsky, l. moholy-nagy and josef albers, to invite them to exhibit their work at the galleria del milione, which ensued in their one-man shows during 1934 and '35 when vordemberge-gildewart also had a show at that gallery, marinetti welcomed in his opening speech the refugee-artists 'coming from the north' where their existence had become impossible by the nazi-regime. when mr. and mrs. gropius visited me in milan, then coming from london, i arranged a meeting with the whole group of modern architects in milan, resulting in a special number of 'domus' about walter gropius. marcel breuer and herbert bayer visited me also, and met my friends.

under the pressure of the 'sanctions' applied to italy in their war in ethiopia, in 1936, sponsored at the league of nations by england, the abovementioned liberal attitude changed to a national block behind mussolini, in memoriam of the bloody colonial expansion of the british empire. when an invitation reached me from black mountain college to join albers and to teach there, i was glad to go, after marrying irene von debschitz who had joined me from berlin. we had to submit to a grilling by the american consul in naples, who was suspicious as to my purpose at bmc, possibly as a policital agent – it is true, bmc was, strangely, known in europe as the 'red college', as i found out to my own surprise – but an assistant and interpreter later apologized to us on account of the ordeal, explaining the strict immigration-laws and also mentioning that he had a friend at bmc, john evarts. my fury called off, but the grilling had been such that i almost decided to stay: keep your america for yourself, who wants to go there and get murdered on fire escape ladder like in your movies, or to live in misery as depicted in them!

this had been the impression, but it was quite different when we came to new york where we enjoyed warm hospitality, and after we arrived in black mountain on september 25, 1936.

materially, we were reduced to the utmost minimum – one thousand five hundred dollars salary a year, one thousand for the second year. but we could live in freedom – to an extent at least.

my first encounter with the whole college was at a seminar i was to hold the following Saturday morning, about albers' paintings which were exhibited in the lobby of lee hall. i compared albers' work with the transparence of components. my school-english caused repeated interruptions in my lecture, to specify certain definitions under the assistance of students and faculty members. my english was still raw, but as i spoke german, french and italian, i was rotated at meals from one table to another where these languages were spoken for practicing purposes.

when i asked albers, which subjects i was to teach beside drawing and painting (or color), i was given free choice. i also was given a 10-day period to get acquainted with the liberal arts program, traditionally unknown in europe. realizing that the atmosphere at black mountain was favorable to experimentation, i thought why not get at 'total experience'? had not my slumbering plans from eleven years before, at the bauhaus in dessau, laid a foundation for this undertaking?

thus, a 'stage studies' course was introduced, with the following outline:

> this course is not intended as training for any particular branch of the contemporary theatre but rather as a general study of fundamental phenomena: space, form, color, light, sound, music, movement, time, etc. the studies take place on the stage for several reasons: it is by nature a place of illusion; it is well suited for representation of the sensibilities of today and for training in the recognition of conscious and visual order; and it is an excellent laboratory for the investigation and illustration of these elements.
>
> the method of study is through active participation and experimentation, improvisation, self-education in mobility on the stage, and presentation to the college of the conclusions arrived at.

in my drawing class i soon realized that most of the students had at most a minimal and very vague knowledge of geometry, which was explained to me as a result of it being a facultative subject in most prep schools. as i wanted to introduce the class into the fascinating subject of PERSPECTIVE, it meant that we had to study geometry first, at least to a degree of primary concepts. i agreed with albers that 'self-expression' in drawing (and painting) was too easy at this stage of studying basic disciplines. from tools and method only a long road leads to expression proper, and in most cases expression is already being mistaken as art! however, drawing and color studied in analogy to euclidian idiom of the ancient greeks become the media for nourishing the searching mind and for developing the skill of the hand.

we were given several rooms at the top floor and a studio at the second floor where the girls had their study rooms and sleeping quarters. the relationship with the faculty members but also with the students was very cordial, and we were introduced in closer fashion at several parties given by anni albers, mrs. dreier, mrs. mangold and by several students. as we were latecomers, this conveyed a feeling of 'belonging'. on our first Sunday, mr. and mrs. rice took us to a day's excursion into the country. the wooded ridges were in full fall colors as we had never seen in europe.

as europeans, we never had any contact with black people, and we became much interested in them, as we were now living with them practically under one roof: the kitchen personnel – jack and ruby – and all the other domestic help. we had dreamed of knowing them and of getting acquainted with their ways and customs. but soon we realized that they drew away into themselves, leaving us with an enigma in spite of their external friendliness and great kindness. ted dreier then explained to me that a plan to enroll black students was frustrated by the fact that the negroes did not want it to happen, and that there were threats they would burn down the building should the plan succeed.

my wife enrolled in albers' werklehre class, also in john rice's plato class and was equally enthusiastic about them. as she had been a professional dress designer in paris and in berlin, mr. rice suggested to her to teach this subject at the college, and in fact, soon many of the girl students and some wives of the teachers appeared in self-tailored evening dresses of which it was said that their cost was not over 90 cents. the course was also taken by some male students, and mr. rice, after attending one of irene's classes, spoke to me in admiration of her ideas and her teaching talent.

my own attendance of one of rice's plato classes convinced me of his profound and subtle method of extracting thought and verbal expression from his students by way of seemingly informal discussions. this i regarded as a sort of parallel to albers' werklehre, even though the subject matter was entirely different. soon some extra-curricular activities developed. there was an interest in a course on <u>architecture</u>, another on <u>typography</u> and <u>printing</u>, both courses of which fell to me. in addition, i became a member of the <u>orchestra</u> as the only cellist, later on to be joined by dante fiorillo, the composer from new york who had come as a guest upon invitation by mr. rice. mr. sly transcribed the trumpet and oboe parts in bach's brandenburg concerti for my soprano-saxophone which i still had from my membership of the bauhaus band and which was muted in various ways in order to fit the timbre. besides the orchestra which sometimes also played under the direction of another guest, mr. surrette, and sometimes under john evarts in his own compositions, a <u>chamber music</u> ensemble was formed to perform music by pur-cell, mozart and beethoven, or to accompany guest performers like the harpsichordist jella pessel, or an alto singer. musical life was very active, the music cottage occupied till late hours by practicing instrumentalists of piano, trombone, violins, clari-net, voices and percussion, streaming out an atonal mixture of disconnected sounds. regular concerts to the whole community crowned these dedicated efforts.

while my course in architecture was limited to basic problems in design and technology, the typography and printing course was expanded to actual printing after my approach to dr. robert l. leslie in new york resulted in his gift of 300 pounds of type and a franklin printing press.

in my <u>stage studies</u> course, to which a sizeable group had enrolled, i began with the definitions of the dimensional rela-tionships on the stage, by first presenting the theoretical elabo-rations i had done at the bauhaus in 1925 and which had been also basic material when i taught stage design at the bauhaus in 1928–29. always aware that here we dealt with a non-pro-fessional approach (compared to the purpose at the bauhaus), these introductions served principally for activating of stimu-lating innate talents possibly not yet discovered, and i invited the class to step on the stage proper and to walk out the different dimensions, even to climb vertically on the ladder, first in obvious chaos, then beginning to get organised, and finally resulting in a sort of a s p a c e p l a y with the improvised piano music by john evarts who had joined our group as its music collaborator. in the growing awareness that this space on the stage was a very particular space, volunteers now began to demonstrate their ideas on the subject by choosing a group of 'actors' and by performing with them their own space play to the remainder of the class seated in the auditorium, and using such devices as they found backstage or had prepared especially, and always supported by evarts' music. these impromptu performances, to which only a few minutes were given for preparation, were immediately discussed between audience and actors as to the validity of the message, and sometimes repeated with some improvements suggested from the auditorium, lighting effects were also used, curtains drawn, props applied, and in order to facilitate acting, alike training suits were worn and masks of neutral expression put over the face. the discharge from face control opened up the key for body control and general mobility which sometimes had proved frustrated, and the uniform clothing helped in bringing out p e r s o n a l i t y of the individual. one female student even came to me to confess that all her life she had an inferiority complex on account of a crooked spine she was born with, and that she now had learned to overcome this feeling by better control with the help of the mask.

thus, like in the above example, such subjects were taken up in a similar explorative way as FORM, COMPOSITION IN SPACE, COLOR AND COLOR COMPOSITION, OPTICS, SOUND, LANGUAGE, NOISE, MUSIC, RHYTHM, POETRY, SPACE-TIME, NUMBERS, THE DREAM, BUILDING, ARCHITECTURE, BUILDING MATERIALS, and ILLUSION.

as the class was composed of members of all disciplines, opinions on the above subjects differed according to scientific, artistic or sociological and other consideration, and complex solutions had to be worked out in order to illuminate and to express on the stage <u>theatrical demonstrations</u> of validity. study groups were formed for research on special fields, and from time to time <u>teachers</u> on various subjects invited to give brief introductory lectures to the class in connection with the plays.

prof. zeuch, for example, lectured on 'time' as a factor in sociology, and ted dreier spoke to the class about 'time' as seen in physics. another point of view was presented by bob goldenson, professor of philosophy, from a more universal point of view. my own prepared lecture to the whole college on 'vision', with projected illustrations, also touched upon the 'time' element in connection with the historically conditioned changes of space concepts and other phenomena.

concepts and plays were gradually worked out to perfection and grouped in a continuous flow to four parts – optics (seeing), acoustics (hearing), building (architecture, symphony), and illusion (metaphysical aspects). a first performance, consisting of the first two subjects, was performed to the whole community at thanksgiving eve, 1936, and the whole performance took place at the end of the term in the spring of 1937. the first presentation was introduced by the LIGHT ORGAN performances by beverly coleman and another student, after they had constructed the large apparatus under my direction.

visitors to the college frequently attended the stage studies classes on suggestion of mr. rice, and also the final rehearsals at times. i remember in particular the visits of the director of the cummington school for music and art, the director of sarah lawrence college, several students from moholy's 'new bauhaus' in chicago, and mr. and mrs. aldous huxley who then lived in california.

the extremely difficult timing of separate group rehearsals towards the end of the term was worked out by mrs. mangold in conjunction with the maze of curricular activities of the individual students, john evarts and myself.

while the two performances were named 'stage studies I' and 'stage studies II', later on i summarized the contents in a script entitled 'PLAY, LIFE, ILLUSION' (SPECTODRAMA) which since then has been published in french (1949), in german (zurich 1960), in english (1952 aspen, 1969 cambridge, 1971 n.y.u.) in spanish (buenos aires 1953) and now in italian (milan 1973), together with an outline 'contemporary studies' as a theoretical basis for spectodrama.

a futile attempt on my part was made to introduce a weekly SILENT DAY at the college during which everybody wears the identical mask and will communicate outside of class rooms by gestures only instead of by words. the suggestion was not approved by the faculty meeting. another suggestion at a faculty meeting, to invite architects gropius and breuer after lake eden was bought and needed planning, also met with silence, though i had felt that albers would support the idea. i subsequently took it upon myself to measure up lake eden, with my students' help, to draw a situation plan containing the existing buildings around the lake, and to design in preliminary form a college building for appr. 200 students and faculty members, presented twelve drawings showing certain interiors of community rooms, class rooms and studies, as well as a view of the whole building and its relationship to the territory. these plans i regarded as a basis for discussion in order to arrive at a PROGRAM for planning lake eden for future use. i visualized the participation of the whole college in an architectural program as a curricular activity. such a program should reflect the needs from different quarters and offer an opportunity for every individual to school himself in responsible thinking.

after having been given an opportunity of presenting my project to the whole college community in an evening lecture with the plans projected by our epidiascope, pointing out the above purpose of the project, i visited lawrence kocher in new york at my next trip north, and asked him to support the gropius-breuer choice as architects by writing to bmc where he knew ted dreier in person. kocher had published some work i had done in 1930 in europe, in his magazine 'the architectural record' of which he was the editor. himself being an architect, he responded sympathetically to my request, especially as he had a high regard for both gropius and breuer.

subsequently, gropius was invited to an informal visit at black mountain, and introduced at a faculty party with that infallible red bordeaux from california (by the gallons) [. . .] he afterward became terribly sick, he whom i knew as one of the most resistant drinkers anywhere.

in the meantime, mr. rice's opinion about my preliminary plans seeped through to me: this was not the kind of college building he himself would favor, at such a formidable scale. also, the style was too modern for his taste. he probably was not aware of a procedure in planning – to draw a large project in order to wind up eventually with one half the size!

the anonymous money donors for sure had been engaged to the utmost for the acquisition of lake eden. on and off mr. rice reported to the student body about his money-raising trips north, in part rather successful, to the astonishment and admiration of all. it was said that people responded to his directness in posing our problems, and to his personality in general.

while in the summer of 1937 several cottages belonging to lee hall but located at a good distance from it were put at the disposal of faculty members who wanted to stay for their vacation, we remained there for about two months during which i painted. albers stayed too with anni, but then they went to mexico. i had an invitation to teach at the cummington school mentioned earlier, and we undertook our first car trip to massachusetts in the old buick which jim king had sold me for 35 dollars and which i had packed to the rim with our stage equipment, figurines, masks, etc., as there would not have been enough time during a summer session to produce it there. at cummington i proceeded in similar fashion as at our stage studies course, though it was here with determined professional musicians and painters or sculptors which made up the student body. again, before we left, a performance of the conclusions arrived at took place before an audience of invited guests and friends of the school.

the rest of the summer vacation we spent at marion, mass., where gropius had rented a house on the sound and had invited us to stay with them, with breuer, and moholy-nagy who came from chicago. it was there that moholy asked me to come to chicago to teach after the next school term in bmc, that is in the fall of 1938, and to formulate a program about my intended form of teaching. however, i felt too much engaged with the work at black mountain to give him a positive answer.

my second year at bmc began with a lecture in which i presented to an enlarged stage studies class the poetry, and the paintings by holbein, of the <u>dance of death</u>, as an <u>example</u> of a morality play from the middle ages reflecting social structure of those times confronted with one single absolute concept: death. by way of this introduction i intended to illustrate a factum of the past and at the same time open up a road for an <u>analogy</u> which shall occupy us hence – to formulate on the stage <u>today's</u> sociological concept analogous to our previous work, and to find the 'absolute' of our own time confronting it. this part had been left out in our previous work, but while i felt a strong need to tackle this task, the majority of the new class was so deeply impressed by the presented material (to most of the students unknown), that the general consensus favored a <u>modernisation</u> of the medieval round dance and outvoted me in my effort to insist on an entirely new venture. thus, our place of action now became the gym which was more suited for a dance in the round, similar to the original plays which usually were performed on the market place in front of the cathedral.

personally not too happy about the course of events of giving <u>alteration</u> precedence over <u>invention</u>, i consoled myself with the fact that the class had taken <u>initiative</u>. i realized, too late, that the enthusiasm of most of the novices in the class had become trapped by my account of the historical dance from europe.

while i had lived next to it – the holbein presentations are in basle where i was born and grew up – all of this was unknown in the NEW WORLD and, like other treasures abroad, arouses the curiosity and interest of the american. the <u>analogy</u> was not understood by the newcomers who had no insight into our previous approach towards creative attempts in our work, and instead pleaded for <u>imitation</u>! to make up for the loss, i later wrote and illustrated a scenario, MONDO NOVA, the sociological complement to PLAY, LIFE, ILLUSION.

a whole year went by with designing, tailoring, constructing, rehearsing, music, translating texts into modern english from the old french version, declamation and dancing. death was presented by bela martin who turned out to become a dynamic and inspiring dancer. in the end, practically the whole college became involved; john evarts' orchestra score was played by the full orchestra under allan sly. for the performance, 3 rows of benches were erected amphitheatrically around a large circle in which the action took place and which was illuminated by one single spotlight from high above. the audience was clothed into identical masks and cloaks and became a uniform wall of individuals without recognizable identity, thus becoming a part of the spectacle. the performance had been posted in many places with a poster THE DANCE MACABRE and had attracted not only the usual audience from black mountain village and asheville but also from the farms and mountains. as the deep silence in which the audience sat created an enormous tension, because of a breakdown of the electrical transformers for bmc spotlight had to be replaced by <u>candles</u> placed around the circle. the performance began in this magic light, but alas! the juice returned soon and everything took its course.

during that school year the scene of college life became troubled with <u>unrest</u> and rivalry in the ranks of the faculty members. in time it became obvious that my friend albers was behind it and got the support of rice's closest friends, dreier and bob wunsch. the action went against john rice, the rector.

although i could never doubt the idealistic motives in albers, i could not understand why two different minds should not exist in this academic forum under one and the same roof, especially between two strong personalities. my inquiries with albers left me with only vague indications. i abhorred political makeshift for attaining power, and whatever the reasons were, my observations caused me suffering and dissatisfaction. i distrusted bob wunsch and ted dreier's character, for not achieving a compromise. as it looked to me, the founder of the college was kicked out! the tragedy played secretly, there was no open action among the community. during these developments i got a letter from moholy-nagy in which he offered me a five-year contract with a 5000 dollar salary per annum. he also described the opportunity of drawing talented students from the university of chicago student body and getting the collaboration among their teachers for my spectodrama venture. in addition, i was to teach a number of professional subjects at the 'new bauhaus', alongside with herbert bayer, jean helion and alexander archipenko whom he also had invited to teach there the following year. and he urged me to send in my program as he was preparing the curricular outline for publication.

i had to make a decision. i loved black mountain, our relationship with students and faculty, our secluded life on top of a mountain where one could work in comparative solitude and where one could roam through the well stacked library and r e a d , a luxury which i had missed in the passed years. here were the students who searched something they would not find in the glamorous universities with their impressive diplomas, harvard, yale, princeton, etc., opening doors to 'success'. instead of success, here there was the search for the t r u t h .

but under the continuous stress of the <u>conflict</u> i resigned from bmc and sent in my 'program' after showing it to dr. moellenhoff who called our group work 'a living philosophy'. albers was great, he did not hold my decision against me, though he had brought me here and always supported my work.

in the interim, gropius and breuer called me to cambridge to work with them on the competition for the pennsylvania world's fair pavilion in 1939. we won, and while the project got into flux, i also won the competition for the north carolina pavilion with my design, bringing me back to north carolina, this time to the state house, museums and kitty hawk. two of my former students from bmc, hendrickson and beverly coleman, became my assistants in the realisation of the two projects.

[added in pen:]

oggebbio, lago maggiore,
march 7, 1973

xanti schawinsky[34]

Slight Song

I write you
now, as the current goes—

we spoke of land when sea
was silent,

and gave history its shape:
a column of air.

Those dense beating drums
you left unwritten,

skin   stretched   across
continents,
over seas.

Seems a secret touch.

Lay this down now, lay this
down—

you swim out of memory
to the rock

where your safety was
for me

at the *outside of knowing.*

New York City

[sound]

You died and teach us the same lesson.
You seem a cathedral,
celebrant of the spring
which shivers for me among the long black trees.

William Carlos Williams, *Spring and All* (1923)

Everywhere: **snow**.

The New York City blizzard of 2010 covered Manhattan in thick drifts of frozen white, impossible to pass. Taxis and buses were left abandoned in the middle of the street. Hundreds of people took shelter in subway stations, waiting on trains that would never arrive.

I had flown from Dublin to New York and met my mother in an Upper East Side rented apartment. Christmas was her favourite holiday, a time when our eternal differences half-disappeared in the anonymity of that great, teeming city, which was not our own.

Of course her roots were rural. Winters frozen twice as bad as this blizzard, in wide-open flat fields of North Dakota. She had left as soon as adulthood came upon her, first for Colorado, then back to Minnesota, and finally to the warmth of Arizona and California, where I was born in November of 1987.

New York always feels a secret source of vitality. And in that spirit we left the apartment, heading for a restaurant in the West Village, which – by recommendation – we simply had to try. The blizzard hadn't hit yet. The air was cold but still. We debated for half a minute whether or not to keep our reservation, before flagging a taxi and driving downtown.

The meal was simple and delicious. A small Italian place, family run, nearly empty on account of the coming weather. We sat, talked and drank happily, unaware of the gathering storm out the window. When we finished, alone in the restaurant, and walked out, the opposite side of the street could not be seen. Sheets of snow fell heavily, burying curbs and parking meters. My first few steps out the door sank knee-deep into the street, no demarcation between the footpath and the road. We hailed cabs with no success, until one finally stopped, asked us where we were going, and drove off when he heard *Upper East Side*.

So we trudged. Through snow above our knees. My mother all the while laughing, *isn't this fun!* No, I thought. No, it isn't...

Her ability to force joy out of sheer misery annoyed me as each step sank deeper into white-covered downtown avenues.

We made it to a subway station. Crowds had gathered there, perhaps as foolish as we had been to ignore warning upon warning from weather men, *not to go outside, not tonight.*

But wasn't the dinner lovely? She said. *I just loved that little place.*

In Bottineau, she remembered, *that would have been nothing. You should see winters in Bottineau!*

But I just loved that little place. Loved it, didn't you?

My mother, Lynette Creasy, was born in a small North Dakota town in November of 1947, daughter of a 'mixed' family of Icelanders and Norwegians. Her father's name was Sigurd Sigurdson. She had me late, at forty, and my brother is a full decade older than I am. Along with my father, a retired academic at the University of California, Los Angeles, they all made strong impressions as teachers, as *guides.*

Life was never easy with my mother. She was erratic, with volatile emotions that would swing from laughter to violence in nearly an instant.

But she was a born teacher – did it all her life. The classroom was her stage, where she became more lively, excited, and generous than anywhere else. At the service after her death, in a church just steps from the beach in Santa Monica, CA, nearly a thousand people came to pay respects. Some were family, but many more were former students and colleagues. Men in their forties approached me, told me they recognised me from back when I was a baby, or a toddler, growing up in the Day Care centre at Brentwood School where my mother was head of the English department.

Her honours American literature course quite literally changed the lives of many who made it through. The final assessment was a months-long group research project on Herman

Melville's *Billy Budd*. Years later, when I came to study literature at Trinity College Dublin, I thought back on the rigour of that experience, our reckoning with Melville, and I thought of how damned lucky we had all been. These days, over drinks with old friends, *Billy Budd* still elicits fear, awe, and considerable joy.

Our relationship was not perfect, not by any means. My mother and I were, for long periods, living together on our own. Not all those memories are pleasant. Some are terrible. Yet when I think back now, from Ireland and a life away, I recall her fierce intelligence, her fearlessness in the face of all authority, and the education she gave me – not just in a school classroom (in fact, rarely there, as I myself bristled under authority), but in the theatres, concert halls, and jazz clubs she took me into. As a tiny child, I was expected to be an adult, cultured and caring. Lessons I am still learning.

She knew little of Black Mountain. My study of the place coincided with her death, not her life. But she was the first to put Emerson into my hands, the first to champion Thoreau, Hawthorne, and Melville. These are the masters who led to my future discoveries.

She died at a wedding party outside Paris, as happy as she probably ever had been. My flight to France was scheduled for the very next day.

We returned to California for the funeral service. (Is it a funeral if there is no coffin, no corpse? Just ashes packed away waiting transit from France.) In her office I discovered copies of every letter I had ever sent home, stacked up neatly, worn and read.

I am writing a letter, though
I do not know where I will send it,
not yet. First it must take form,
announce what it's *about*, if there
is such a thing as about. What am I
saying? What questions will I put
to you? How may I expect you
sometime to respond? In North Dakota,
winter temperatures drop to fifty
degrees below zero with wind-chill.
In 1955 they installed the first traffic
light in our town. Pulling out of the driveway
I plowed the car right into the
only other driver within maybe five miles.
My father bred horses and raced them in
chariots. He died from hospital error.
Nobody in the family saw it fit then
to take action. We remember his drinking,
his smile. My sons' faces are his face.
They race now in chariots, breathing fire.
I am writing a letter, though
I do not know yet where I will send it.

     Can I look forward to your reply?
     Do you have my address—

In November of 2014, I climbed the stairs to a fifth-floor walk-up in Greenwich Village. The walls of the tiny apartment were covered with photographs of Black Mountain College. Just above a small, cluttered desk, the image of the summer arts institute, with Dreier, Gropius, the Alberses, all the rest, lined up either side of a tree by the lake. The apartment belongs to Mary Emma Harris. Since the late 1960s, she has compiled thousands of documents, recordings and biographies, assembling an indispensable image of the place in her book, *The Arts at Black Mountain College*, published the year I was born, 1987.

1946 summer arts faculty, Lake Eden
Courtesy of the Western Regional Archives, State Archives of North Carolina

Here we get into the mythology of Black Mountain College. We have to be very careful.

Recorder clicks . . . counting . . .

I'm Mary Emma Harris. We're in New York City. The date is November 17, 2014.

Now everything dates itself. I started recording my interviews in 1970, and nothing dated itself . . . It was pre-digital . . .

Where were you living at that stage?

I'm from North Carolina. I grew up on a small farm near the coast. My mother raised six children on my grandfather's farm. So we didn't have a sophisticated background. No city in our background. More sweet potato and beans, and cabbage and carrots and cows. Tobacco, of course.

I went from there to Greensboro College, a small Methodist school. I'd worked all my life; once I had my degree, it didn't occur to me I should get a job.

A friend and I decided we were going to go to Europe. So we took a freighter, the Black Heron, over, and worked at Neckermann in Frankfurt. It was a horrible job, dreadful. You had to be there early in the morning. It was dark when you left, and it was dark when you came home.

We were six Americans filling the English orders.

Then I taught in the Berlitz School in Wiesbaden. I'm from the South, so I say 'Ah' – you know, 'Ah do this, and Ah do that.' Somebody said, 'Go show them your English teaching certificate and don't say "Ah!"'

So I got the job. It was fun. There were people from all over

Europe teaching there. We were young. We had a devilish time. When I came back to the States, I didn't have any money. I had to get a job. They were integrating the schools, starting with teachers. A friend of my family, someone my mother's age, had gone to the black junior high school, so I went and taught Art and English there for two years. And then to Chapel Hill to study Art History. That's when I first heard about Black Mountain.

This was in 1968–1969. Nothing was known then about this college. The head of my department had told people – which made sense – that they couldn't do a thesis on Black Mountain because it was all hearsay. I know from doing interviews how inaccurate hearsay and memory can be.

Then I learned – which the head of the department should have known – that the college papers were in Raleigh, at the State Archives, just twenty minutes away. So I started going over whenever I could and digging in.

At that point the college had basically disappeared from memory, except for the Black Mountain poets because they carried the name 'Black Mountain,' even though it was totally misleading. There were a lot of poets excluded from 'The Black Mountain Poets' who were at the college and people who were never there who were included; the title was really the Olson-Creeley, *Black Mountain Review* group of writers.

People would say, 'Oh yeah, Mary! Black Mountain College, it was an interesting but failed experiment in American education. It closed.'

I really learned not to listen to people at that point.

Where did Black Mountain come from? What was the experiment in the first place?

Well, that's a big question. Essentially, it was part of a much larger picture at the time, of Americans trying to define what an American education should be. American education had really been based on European models. I am not an historian of American education in any sense. But in this country at that time, the fact that education should be universal was exceptional.

The college was in the centre of that effort – the progressive education movement – to define what an education should be in a democratic society: how people could best learn so that they would not just be absorbers, but would be thinkers and activists, and really vital in their society. There was a lot of experimentation at that point in American education, but Black Mountain took it a step further.

Bennington College was founded in 1932 as a progressive college for women. The founders spent several years building buildings, defining their educational ideals. It was a very 'proper' school, with a more open curriculum than conventional American education. Black Mountain, in contrast, was put together in two months. They didn't have time to refine everything. They found this big white wooden building that they could move into. Black Mountain was, really, on the far edge of experimentation at the time. And, of course, central to the college's educational programme was that the arts should be at the centre. Other schools included the arts in the curriculum. But at Black Mountain, everyone took part in the arts. It wasn't just a classroom thing.

I don't think the founders had any idea how this would play out. But the arts really infused the entire community.

Who were those figures from the beginning?

The college was founded by four teachers who had resigned or been fired by President Hamilton Holt. They all had very different backgrounds.

John Andrew Rice, Classics professor who was at the centre of the Rollins fracas, was raised in the South, son of a Methodist preacher. He had, if not an impoverished background, limited financial means. Certainly preachers weren't paid a lot then. His mother died when he was very young, and at one point he and his brother were put in an orphanage.

Theodore Dreier, teacher of mathematics and physics, came from a very prominent Brooklyn family of German descent, very well to do. Very involved with the arts and cultural activities.

Ralph Reed Lounsbury, a lawyer, died a couple of weeks after the college opened, of a heart attack or a stroke.

Frederick Georgia taught chemistry and remained for several years, but he really belonged in a conventional institution. He was not of the same spirit as the others.

But you have to give Lounsbury and Georgia a lot of credit; they stood up to president Hamilton Holt at Rollins and put their jobs on the line, which is admirable. They didn't have to do that. As a consequence, they were fired. So these were the founders, summer of 1933. All of this was happening at the same time Hitler was becoming Chancellor in Germany.

What about the challenges of starting this experiment in the South?

Later, being in the South made a difference. The challenges were not so much being in the South at that point, as they were just the basic issues of how to get students, how to find faculty, how to pay the bills each year. There was no endowment.

It was about how to keep shelter over their heads. The Blue Ridge buildings, a couple of months after they moved in, were sold in bankruptcy proceedings. That voided their contract and they could have been out on the street.

So certainly being in the South played an important role in some ways. But at that early point it wasn't really a concern. Their real concern was survival.

What was it like in those early years? Before the most legend-
ary names, who often didn't spend all that much time at Black
Mountain. And who certainly weren't involved in the founding of
the experiment.

It was a very small community. I think there were nineteen or
twenty students in the first year. By the end of the 1930s, there
were perhaps seventy. The faculty, there were maybe fifteen.
They were the corporation. It was a non-stock corporation with
faculty as members. Sometimes a faculty member's spouse would
teach, or a particularly gifted student would teach.

Faculty and students lived together in Robert E. Lee Hall, a
vast wooden building where YMCA summer conferences were
held. It encouraged a real coherence within the community.
The faculty with children lived in small cottages. Everybody ate
together in the dining hall: faculty and families and students.

They started to farm the first year. Living together, very
closely, they learned very quickly. There were a lot of conflicts
from the beginning. Personality conflicts. Conflicts over ideology. And a lot of time was spent in faculty meetings hammering
these things out.

The faculty didn't vote; they reached decisions by consensus,
which took a long time. It was a small, modest community.

They were aware that they were special, that this was an
experiment. The college immediately drew a number of important visitors: John Dewey, Albert Einstein . . . It had a lot of pub-
licity, from the beginning, with the 'Ruckus at Rollins.' People
in education knew about the college.

It was a quiet community. Hikes in the mountains, often
camping overnight. They did not have that much contact with
the local community, except through the farm. Someone is
doing a lot of work on the farm – David Silver. He's showing
just how much the people working in the farm were involved
with community. But basically the college provided its own

entertainment. John Evarts, who taught music, could improvise anything on the piano. So he would play at dances on Saturday nights. They would have a chorus sing after meals during the week.

Classes were held generally in the mornings and evenings. Afternoons, they had the work programme because a lot of the maintenance was done by students and faculty. So it was intimate, very intensely involved in learning. The arts classes were very important, but the arts were also as a means for entertaining themselves.

And students had a different role than they would in conventional institutions?

Right. There was one student on the Board of Fellows, the administrative body. The faculty made all educational decisions, but the Board of Fellows handled finances. They hired and fired faculty. There was one student member among about seven or eight. There were a lot of community meetings and student meetings. The relationship between student and faculty was very different than in most schools.

Everybody was exposed and vulnerable. The faculty did not teach and then go home in the evening. There was very little privacy.

There were certain barriers – faculty and student – that were broken down at the college. The lines of communication were much more open. But there was a clear division. Faculty were faculty. Students were students.

I was just reading an interview I did, with someone at Black Mountain who considered himself to be a genius. That got in the way throughout his life. But he was right, in that there certainly was an aristocracy at the college. Josef and Anni Albers came in the fall of 1933, from the Bauhaus. They didn't speak English.

So from the beginning there was a German table in the dining hall. Ted Dreier spoke German fluently, and the Dreiers and Alberses became good friends. They had their table, and select students would sit there.

Some felt left out by that sense of aristocracy. Others couldn't have cared less.

It wasn't a perfect, homogeneous community. The European faculty who came were generally far more advanced in their careers than the young Americans who were teaching.

It was not a Utopian community. There were a lot of conflicts, a lot of disagreements. But that was part of the educational process. The students were part of the decision-making process, and they learned that grown-ups don't always get along. There were a lot of different opinions that needed to be sorted out in the community if the community was going to survive.

And the European influence?

I often wonder what the college would have been like if the European faculty had not come. There is no way to know what direction it would have taken. But in the first year they brought Josef and Anni Albers over to teach art and weaving. They brought over Heinrich Jalowetz, who had been conductor of the opera in Cologne. He had been one of Schoenberg's first students, along with Berg and Webern. Refugees were hired in all areas of the general curriculum: mathematics, physics, chemistry, history and social science, theatre, art, psychology.

These were people who had esteemed careers in Europe. They brought an important corrective to what had become a certain academic permissiveness in progressive education. These were people who experienced a very disciplined course of study, and they expected this of their students.

Albers was very opposed to 'self-expression' in art education, for the student, which, of course, was the hallmark of progressive education. *Express yourself.* Albers said that self-expression was a by-product of disciplined study. That came first.

The Europeans gave a structure to the community, as well as a really high standard of intellectual training. The students benefitted from this. People would say, when I started my research: 'The students were just artists. None of them really went to get advanced degrees.' Well, a lot of people went on to get their PhDs, and to teach in universities. They benefitted from the intellectual training that they had at Black Mountain, through the Americans and the Europeans.

One student said she arrived home for Christmas after her first semester at Black Mountain, and she was speaking with a German accent! There was so much German spoken at the college. The refugees also learned English. It was an important place of transition for people.

There was a concern that the college would lose its essential American character if it became too heavily European, which happened during the war, when most of the Americans joined the war effort.

A number of refugees also sent their children to Black Mountain. Word got around that this was a place that welcomed Jewish students. A place where there was a different kind of education than you would find in any other American education system. During the war, this was really a refuge for these people.

What were the Alberses doing there?

Josef Albers was teaching a modified Bauhaus curriculum. He adapted the Bauhaus curriculum, which was for professionals, to general education. He taught colour. He taught design. Painting – basically painting was watercolour, with very large brushes, capturing the form of the image. They did use smaller brushes too. He also taught drawing. Students will tell you that his drawing course was phenomenal. They learned to draw at Black Mountain under Albers. There are wonderful drawings by Albers's students.

Anni Albers taught weaving. She was not initially hired, but she was appointed instructor in the first year. Frederick Georgia built a loom for her. They remained at Black Mountain for sixteen years, largely because they became believers. They believed in the educational ideals of the college. Albers taught several summer sessions at Harvard with Gropius. He saw what Gropius was struggling against there, in terms of trying to create a new curriculum in a very Beaux-Arts traditional school. Had Gropius and Albers been together at Harvard, they would have been a force.

Albers stayed at Black Mountain because he loved it. It was tremendously demanding. Faculty meetings, community life. I think his artwork suffered during those years. He had two sabbaticals, one for a year, and another for a year and a half. That's when he did his most important work. He started painting his concentric squares after he left Black Mountain.

The Alberses were strong forces in the community. He could be very rigid. He knew exactly what he thought was right. As somebody said, the disappointing thing was that he was usually right.

In the first years, the Alberses lived with the other faculty in Lee Hall. At Lake Eden, they shared a house with the Dreier family, to whom they were very close.

Albers was not one of the faculty members who went on hikes with the students, or who was hanging out all the time. He was very private. Any free time he had was spent on his own work. Sometimes students were invited to his studio, but rarely. Yet he was much loved by his students. After the war, many of the GIs didn't want to do the Bauhaus-style exercises. They wanted to be *painters*. So he was constantly being challenged by that group. It's hard to explain how great a force he was in the community.

What starts to change after that early period of the college's founding?

John Rice and Josef Albers were the two dominant figures in the early years, and Ted Dreier. But you can't discount people like John Evarts, who had so much to do with the spirit of the college, or Robert Wunsch, who taught theatre.

In 1937 the college purchased its own property at Lake Eden, north of the village of Black Mountain. The resignation of John Rice, who had been on an extended sabbatical, in February 1940 and the move to Lake Eden in June 1941 marked a turning point in the college's history.

During the war, most of the American men left. It was basically a girls' school, with a few men and a predominantly European faculty. The transition was not deliberate.

In the summer of 1944, the college sponsored the first summer sessions in the arts: a music institute celebrating the seventieth birthday of Arnold Schoenberg and an art institute. The special summer sessions attracted a lot of people in music and the visual arts to the college.

More and more, the college became known for its arts curriculum. Not because it was promoted over other things, but because it was very vibrant and that was drawing students during the summer sessions. It was really the summer sessions that began to turn the college around with a larger focus on the arts.

After the war, the liberal arts curriculum was strong (as it was the whole time, except the last years). It was hard, during the war, when the college community was so small, to have enough faculty. You often couldn't have more than one person in a field. People say 'The Music Department,' and 'The Art Department,' 'The Psychology Department.' When there was only one person, everyone was head of the department.

After the war, the college was able to hire more faculty.

Fortunately, it was approved for the GI Bill. If it had not qualified, it would have closed. Suddenly, a lot of men who were older than the usual out-of-high-school student enrolled. They were more independent.

The college had changed. It was no longer the 1930s focused, very small community. Cliques were probably much stronger at that point. Americans were hired, such as M. C. Richards, who were younger people, who had ideas of their own. They were challenging the status quo. Challenging Albers. Challenging Dreier. Moving the college along to a different point. The postwar years were a contentious period, but a very vibrant period.

In the early years there was a pioneering spirit. They were very self-conscious of being an experiment in American education. After the war, it also was, but I think people took a lot for granted then, in terms of what was required to keep the college going. The GI Bill for the first time provided a steady income. It was just too easy. Then suddenly the number of students on the GI Bill dwindled. Things began to fall apart financially.

Ted Dreier, the primary fundraiser, worked endlessly to raise little bits of money. In his papers in the State Archives, there are these envelopes on which he's scribbled in tiny writing, 'so-and-so: $10,' 'so-and-so: $20.' He would take the bus everywhere just trying to get a few dollars here and there. No one was willing to do that after he left. No one had that type of dedication. Also, he had contacts in the North through his family that other people just didn't have.

The changes that occurred in the college were not planned; it was just inevitable, organic. People were drawn to the strength of the arts.

There is a connection between Black Mountain and the Northeast: New York, Connecticut, etc.

The connection to the Northeast was extremely important. Somewhat, but less so, in California. Many of the students came from the Northeast in the early years.

Most of the money that was raised to support the college came from the Northeast. The William C. Whitney Foundation was the one foundation that gave consistently. In the first summer, Rice was spending a lot of time at the Guggenheim Foundation, where Henry Allen Moe, Director, was very interested in the college. Ted Dreier's contacts were in the Northeast. The progressive education movement was most alive there.

Students would go back to the Northeast – to New York, to Boston – on breaks. Give concerts and talks about the college and pass the hat around to help support the college.

Also, the visitors who came down and gave lectures or concerts were extremely important to this very isolated community, in terms of bringing in new ideas, new blood – even if they were only at Black Mountain for three or four days. Hundreds of people visited the college.

Two of the artists who came from the Northeast at a critical point in their careers were John Cage and Merce Cunningham.

They came to Black Mountain from the Northeast, but their roots were in California and Washington State. I interviewed both of them. They loved Black Mountain. In the spring of 1948, they arrived on this so-called two-person tour. The college said, 'you can come . . . we don't have any money to pay you.' So they were there for several days. The college embraced them. There they found a community of kindred spirits. Many people who came to the college had not encountered that kind of compatibility and acceptance before. Many of the people who were at the college had been outsiders elsewhere.

Cunningham commented that in New York it was so hard to find a space to work in and dance. Students had to hold jobs at the same time they were studying. But at Black Mountain, everything was totally focused. The college had an ability to let things happen. It was not over-programmed. Albers was very good there. He could be very rigid in some ways, but he never told people what to teach when they came. He always said, 'teach what you want to.' He was not a controlling presence in that respect, as some people were. He appreciated the fact that people were there for the summer. They should have some time to relax.

Cage and Cunningham were invited to return for the 1948 summer. Cage said he wanted to have a Satie festival. And the faculty said, great! They didn't have to find an auditorium. At Black Mountain they didn't have to deal with unions. They could focus on the performance.

The highlight was a performance of Erik Satie's *The Ruse of Medusa* (*Le piège de Méduse*). Students and faculty made sets. They made costumes. People joined in as they did for other productions. At that point, it wasn't, 'Okay, we're going to do this performance that will be historically import-ant later.' Everyone was just having a good time. That's how the other performances were done as well. You didn't have a drama department, where only the drama students did things. Everybody just chipped in and did what they could. So Cage and Cunningham loved it. And they came back in the summer of '52, and then Cunningham again in '53. That summer the Merce Cunningham Dance Company was formed at the college. All he had to do that summer was choreograph and teach. It was wonderful.

The summer people had a very different relationship to the college than the people who were there year-round. The summer people weren't part of the corporation. They didn't have to be concerned about raising money, about student issues, about any of the other community problems. For them, it was just a won-derful summer, meeting interesting people, having great con-certs. It was a totally different atmosphere than in wintertime.

In wintertime, life was much more daily. You went to class.

You milked the cows. You brought in the corn. You repaired fences. You debated endlessly what the college should be, what the community should be. Whether or not students were taking responsibility for things they should. Whether the faculty were doing a good job.

The summertime was much lighter. Summertime is beautiful in North Carolina in the mountains. People were out of the cities, where it was hot. People didn't have air conditioning then, in the cities.

Most of the guest artists were not famous then. Now, you think: 'Oh, de Kooning!' We think Kline, Feininger, all these famous people. But at that point, even the refugees – like Feininger or Ozenfant – had to teach or to establish themselves as artists. They didn't have established reputations in this country. They were starting out again, often at an advanced age.

Summer was very different. But if you asked Cage and Cunningham, Black Mountain was a meeting of kindred spirits. The relationship to students was so different. Now, if I go to a university to lecture, I arrive, I'm taken to my hotel room. I have dinner with some faculty. I give my lecture. I may or may not have some chance to talk to the students.

At Black Mountain, when faculty arrived they were immediately drawn into the community. Josef Marx, who was a musician, commented that he was anxious because he didn't know what he would be teaching. The college said: 'Don't worry about it. You'll find out when you get here!' As soon as he arrived, students came to his house and said, 'Let's go for a hike up the mountain.' Students would have little parties in their studies and invite the summer faculty.

Some summer faculty like Feininger didn't teach a formal class. If you didn't want to, you didn't have to.

There was an interaction between artists and media. Most famously,

perhaps, in Cage's 'Happening.' You get a number of different stories
about how that happened and what it actually was.

There is no straight story about that!

Pete Jennerjahn had been teaching a Light Sound Movement Workshop. He taught art, but he also was a jazz musician. In his class there was a lot of drumming and improvisation. They did performances combining dance, movement, and music. They painted on filmstrips and projected the film. This was very modest but not traditional theatre. But unlike the Cage production, they were rehearsed performances.

At the time, M. C. Richards was translating Artaud's *Theatre and Its Double*, and it was being discussed in the New York Black Mountain community including Cage. The idea of a non-didactic theatre was very much on people's minds. Charles Olson, who taught at Black Mountain, was also very interested in non-didactic theatre.

What do I know about the 1952 Cage performance: it was basically created in a day. Cage conceived it in the morning; they performed it that night. As I understand it, Cage gave people time slots that he had determined by using chance operations. The performers could do what they wanted to do. A ladder was set up. There was a piano. There was a phonograph, some paintings. I think Franz Kline's large Black Mountain painting, or Rauschenberg's white or black paintings were hung from the rafters. It took place in the dining hall. M. C. Richards took part as did Charles Olson, Rauschenberg, and Cunningham, among others.

The theatre, as Cage has pointed out, was not a traditional theatre-in-the-round. The seats were in four sections, around a centre where the ladder was. In a theatre-in-the-round, generally you're looking at the centre. In this situation, Cunningham – and the dog that followed him – was moving in and out of the aisles among the audience.

Everyone has a different memory of what happened. That's part of the success of the performance. Everybody had a different view depending on where they were sitting. At the time it wasn't considered to be important. If it had been, everyone would have made photographs and written about it.

We'll never know exactly what happened. People cannot even agree on what to call it or how to spell it: the Happening, Theatre Piece #1 (or Theater Piece #1), Untitled Event.

Here we get into the mythology of Black Mountain College. We have to be very careful. Albert Einstein visited the college for an afternoon. Nathan Rosen, who had taught at the college and was a nuclear physicist, was teaching at the university at Chapel Hill at that point. He asked Einstein if he'd like to see the college. This was on Sunday, April 27, 1941. His visit is described in a bulletin of the time. People recall he was there for days. Must have been a jam-packed afternoon!

One amusing story: one condition Einstein insisted on was that no one could take photos of him. He didn't want this to be a photo opportunity for the college. He didn't want to be used. A group was walking with him on a ridge and saw a family taking pictures. And all the students were hoping someone would take a picture of the group walking with Einstein!

They didn't.

You have to be careful with Black Mountain. The Happening was probably not as extravagant as people have come to think. It was really very simple and modest. Some people thought it was just nothing. Johanna Jalowetz commented that this was like the Dark Ages! One person decided that if all the ambient sounds like frogs, etc., were part of the performance, he would rather just go outside and listen to the frogs and crickets.

And then we move to a period where Olson was in charge, and writing becomes a central focus of the college.

In 1949, the college really had no financial means. The GI Bill student enrollment was dwindling, and the 1930s sources had dried up. Dreier was trying to find a solution. He was investigating a number of possibilities. One idea was to focus on the arts, which had become – realistically – the strongest part of the curriculum.

There was a lot of paranoia at the college. They thought Dreier might try to give the college away, which he couldn't do legally. A number of people turned on him, and he was asked to resign from the Board of Fellows, not the faculty. He left, and both Alberses left in protest. Most of the European arts faculty left in protest.

Edward Dahlberg was invited to teach in 1948–49 when M. C. Richards was on sabbatical. After a couple of weeks he fled back to the city! He recommended Charles Olson, who was living in Washington, D.C., then. Olson commuted one weekend a month to teach. He remained for the 1949 summer session. Then he left for the Yucatan and didn't return to Black Mountain until the summer of 1951.

Olson was a very strong presence. Students were awaiting his return. Even in his absence, he was a strong presence.

In those years, the early 1950s, the college became an art school by attrition.

They didn't have much money. They were already selling land to keep going. There were very few faculty in the general curriculum.

Even though literature became much more important to the college in the 1950s, it was really a very interactive community with dance and painting and music. Joseph Fiore, a former student, was teaching painting, and there was a very active group of painters there. There were dancers. Katherine Litz taught one academic year and three summers.

There were as many painting students as literature students. People were painting and writing and dancing. You weren't just involved in one area of the arts.

Olson was the dominant figure, both in physical size and personality. Especially in the last three years, he was the centre of the college. Though it wasn't until 1953 that he became rector. After 1949 no one wanted to be 'rector.' Instead there were chairmen of the faculty and Board of Fellows. The 'rector' was the person everyone would go after! So for a while the college was leaderless.

That brings us to the end of the story, when Olson is responsible for closing the college.

The college became smaller and smaller. After the summer of 1953, the college moved into the faculty cottages up the hill and the lower campus with the dining hall, studies building, and lodges was abandoned. As Michael Rumaker and others said, it was really a kind of psychically crazy place in those times. There were no drugs as we know them today. I think there were some prescription uppers or whatever. Someone said Creeley brought some marijuana. That was really exotic at the time. There was alcohol. Boy, there was a lot of alcohol.

The lower campus was rented to the people who eventually bought the property and turned it into a camp.

In the fall of 1956, essentially there were only three faculty: Olson in literature, Wesley 'Wes' Huss in drama, and Joe Fiore in painting. Fiore was taking a year's sabbatical. So they really had three faculty, one of whom was on sabbatical. Olson and Huss decided it was time to close the Lake Eden campus, but not necessarily to close the college.

Olson always had big ideas, new visions of what the college might be, which he could not implement. In the fall of 1956 he conceived of the college as a 'dispersed university' with activities all over the United States, maybe all over the world. A few people would remain at Lake Eden to keep a core presence. Olson gave his *Special View of History* lectures in the winter of 1957 in San Francisco, as part of the Black Mountain curriculum.

Robert Duncan, who had taught theatre for the spring and summer term in 1956, continued to work on his Medea plays in San Francisco with Black Mountain students who had moved there. This was part of Olson's 'dispersed university.'

Before September 1950, if there was not enough money to pay the meagre faculty salaries, at the end of the year the unpaid salaries were dismissed as a debt against the college. After 1950, unpaid salaries or 'contingent salaries' were listed, and the debt mounted over the years. Three former faculty – women who were older, who left with no retirement – including Hazel Larsen, who was disabled by polio, brought a suit against the college, with the encouragement of some Black Mountain alumni. They wanted the contingent salaries to be paid. They wanted the college, if it was going to close, to close respectably, with all debts paid.

In March 1957 a judge ordered the college to cease academic programs until all debts were paid. That really was the end of the college. Olson was executor and the college closed respectably. He found a place for the library. He found a place for the looms. All debts including contingent salaries were paid and the books were closed with a balance of zero. That was really the end of Black Mountain College. And it was time.

After that, it began to live a new life. Your work has been a key in telling that story. If that was the life of the college, what's been the afterlife?

After 1957, for many years the college was forgotten, except the Black Mountain poets – Olson, Creeley, Duncan, and the people published in the *Black Mountain Review*. Most people just dismissed it as an interesting but failed experiment in American education. After all, it did close.

When I started doing my research in 1968, at Chapel Hill, there was very little known. I would ask people, and they would say: 'Oh yeah, Black Mountain College. It died.'

The first thing that really brought the college to the attention of the general public, or the academic public, was Martin Duberman's book, 1972, *Black Mountain: An Exploration in Community*. He focused on the college as a community. How it worked and how it didn't work. This was a major publication by a major scholar. That did begin to bring some attention.

My book followed in 1987. It took me a long time!

Duberman's book focused on the community history, conflicts and ideals; mine, more on the arts within the context of the educational philosophy.

Bit by bit, interest in the college grew. The founding of the Black Mountain Museum + Arts Center in Asheville has been extremely important. They've sponsored exhibitions, colloquia, and all kinds of events.

For many the college has now taken on mythic dimensions. It has become a symbol of the importance of arts in the academic experience, and of academic freedom, even for people who don't really know anything about the college. For a lot of people it has become a touchstone.

I could never have imagined in 1968–69 that the college would have assumed such an important position in the arts and education. The stellar members of the community – both faculty and students – have drawn attention to the college. People forget that Ruth Asawa, Robert Rauschenberg, Ray Johnson, Susan Weil, Dorothea Rockburne, Viola Farber, Kenneth Snelson, Michael Rumaker, and many others were just students at the college. Events such as Albers's curriculum and the college as heir to the Bauhaus ideals, the founding of the Merce Cunningham Dance Company, the 'Happening,' Buckminster Fuller's first dome, and the accomplishments of many students – only about 1200 attended in twenty-four years – have placed the college in the lexicons of the history of art in the United States in the twentieth century.

Despite the incredible accomplishments, the college still is not that well known except in limited arts and education circles.

There's so much to be learned from Black Mountain. For people who study the college, who become involved with it, it has a real transformative force. It certainly did for me.

It does for other people too.

It was a very courageous little place. A creative place. A courageous, creative *little* place. But it was not easy.

One thing we didn't talk about is that Olson and Creeley had this enormous correspondence. (You know more about this than I do.) They corresponded almost every day. They began to build a community of writers: Cid Corman and *Origin* magazine. They figured they could handle Cid and have him publish what they wanted him to, but no! He had his own ideas.

Jonathan Williams was starting his Jargon publications. They thought he might be somebody they could handle. No! Jonathan had his own ideas.

So they started the *Black Mountain Review*, over which they would have total control. Robert Duncan was very important in that triumvirate. And then there were a lot of people never actually at Black Mountain, but whose work was published in the *Review* who became part of that intellectual, poetic Black Mountain community.

This is something that was part of Black Mountain, but wasn't a part. It was a community of Olson, Duncan, and Creeley exchanging letters. The *Review* was actually printed in Majorca. The community of artists, writers, poets, and painters was really important to the college: the exchange between them.

I've been at this since 1968, and it's an endlessly fascinating place. One thing that has been extremely important is the people who were there. They're such interesting people. Their lives have taken such interesting paths.

The real mystery is the dynamics of a community, just how that evolved. And also how it can influence our own education today. The arts were not just taught at the college, they infused the entire community. There is a lot of information now about how important to the learning experience the arts can be, from preschool through university teaching. And yet it's rarely employed. The arts still have to fight for a place in the curriculum.

One other thing that students say was very important: they didn't have grades. Grades were recorded in the office for transfer purposes, but students didn't know what they were. So they studied harder, they said. They weren't just studying for a test. They were studying for the pleasure of learning. There is so much we could learn today.

Large universities obviously can't be Black Mountain, but they could learn a lot from Black Mountain that could be incorporated into a traditional program.

Black Mountain wasn't an easy place to be. People were challenged constantly. People arrived and immediately other students said, 'What do you do?' – not 'What do you know,' but 'What do you do?'

Black Mountain was a very challenging place.

Dakota Dream (unsung)

Sound, sense – imploring; that those who go here
go where wind once shook our cities.
Laughter, learning, distinction:
distraction for the bored and deadly boring.
Writing books, a doubled edge –
No use (she knew) to take the pledge.

But I who walk here, and friends beside,
hidden go among them.
Tried, time-tested – timorous behind the eyes.
You (as the glow-worm lighted as it dies)
find truth in talk,
believe credentialed lies.

Welter in civilized life,
the voices of children removed & undone.
Grace sure takes its liberties with the young.
Water to wash you, wake you with sound in soft pitch –
Keep this music close to heart & to hand;
sing the Lake & River below the Bridge.

OFFICE MEMORANDUM   UNITED STATES
                              GOVERNMENT

                              DATE: 6/26/56

TO: DIRECTOR, FBI

FROM: SAC, CHARLOTTE (17-942)

SUBJECT: BLACK MOUNTAIN COLLEGE,
           BLACK MOUNTAIN, N.C.
           VAM

Re Bulet June 8, 1956 and Charlotte letter to Bureau, 5/31/56.

This matter was referred to this office by VARO, Winston-Salem, North Carolina, upon the completion of its Summary Compliance Survey of Black Mountain College.

On June 6, 1956 a preliminary conference was held with United States Attorney JAMES M. BALEY, JR., Western District of North Carolina, Asheville, North Carolina. Mr. C. E. HEMINGWAY, Chief of Vocational Rehabilitation and Education Division, and CECIL PATE, Chief Attorney, VARO, Winston-Salem, North Carolina were present with SA _____ during the discussion.

Mr. PATE explained to Mr. BALEY that monthly certification of training, VA Form VB7-1996B, had been submitted to the Veterans Administration by the subject and the veterans for each month of attendance by the veteran at the college and that these certificates showed no absences of veterans except in one instance. Mr. PATE further explained that enrollment certificates, VA form 71999, had been submitted by the College on each veteran setting up a proposed course of study and indicating that the veteran had been in attendance five or six hours per day on five or six days per week. Mr. PATE stated that these documents were the basis on which the Veterans Administration relied in making subsistence payments to the veterans.

Mr. PATE stated that he felt that the information reported in the Compliance Summary Report raised a doubt as to the accuracy and truthfulness of the information to the Veterans Administration in the two documents described above.

Mr. HEMINGWAY stated that this matter had been discussed with officials of the College and that they claimed they had complied in substance with the provisions of these documents but had indicated that they did not comply in detail in that their scheduling of classes was on an irregular basis.

Mr. HEMINGWAY advised that the College had been re-approved for Veterans Administration students on a limited basis by the North Carolina Department of Education as a result of a conference held on June 6, 1956 between officials of the College, representatives of the state, and the Veterans Administration. The approval was limited to completion by the veterans presently enrolled in their courses. Mr. BALEY stated that it was his opinion that this was a matter which could in all probability be better handled by administrative action taken by the Veterans Administration. However, he suggested that a preliminary investigation be made to see if any evidence of intent to furnish false information could be developed. Mr. BALEY requested that he be kept advised of developments as the investigation proceeded so that he could determine whether or not he would contemplate prosecution.

On June 20 and 21, 1956, three of the veterans were interviewed and advised that they had received instruction equalling or exceeding the amount indicated on their respective certificates of enrollment and that they had no absences from classes which had not been made up. They each stated they knew of no attendance records being kept by the school but explained that the total enrollment was only about 26 students and that absences would have been noticed if there had been any.

_____, treasurer of Black Mountain College, Black Mountain, North Carolina, advised on June 21, 1956 that he realized that the enrollment certificates indicated that five or six hours of instruction per day for five or six days per week were to be furnished to the veterans. He said he knew that this instruction had not been given on a regular basis of five or six hours per day but that all veterans received at least 30 hours per week of instruction. He stated that he was orally informed by Veterans Administration representatives at the outset of the program that 30 hours of instruction per week was what was required, and that in submitting the enrollment certificates he arbitrarily allotted this time on a five or six hours per day five or six days per week basis. He stated that he had no intention of misleading the Veterans Administration or of furnishing false information to it.

_____ advised that there has been no attendance records kept by Black Mountain College in the past. He exhibited a form which he said had been agreed upon between himself and the Veterans Administration for recording attendance in the future.

Investigation determined that all veterans except three who have been interviewed are presently residing at addresses which are outside the Charlotte Division while on summer vacation.

Mr. BALEY stated that he felt that the requirements of attendance established by the documents mentioned above were non-specific and indefinite and that any effort to prove non-compliance could be successfully met by the claim that substantial compliance was had even though the compliance was not on a regular basis. He states that it would be necessary to show the facts indicating that a student was not in the College during a long period of time in order to prove a case against the College. He felt that the facts developed thus gave no indication that such was the case and, therefore, stated that he believed no further investigation was necessary.

Since those veterans not yet interviewed are presently outside this Division and since the United States Attorney has indicated he does not contemplate prosecution, no additional investigation is being conducted. A closing report will be submitted.

Black Mountain is a living example
of democracy in action.

John Dewey

No Art

Throw up your hands
                    dancer—

Here's a plane & field
                    of your own;

                Shift of light, so she dances

                        in shadow:

                        seeking action, not
                        gratification

Yearling, by Astrid Kaemmerling
(in correspondence with the author)

Dublin

[design]

When I first read Le Corbusier's claim, 'a house is a machine for living in,' I was struck immediately by a parallel poetic revelation. In his introduction to *The Wedge* (1944), William Carlos Williams writes:

> There's nothing sentimental about a machine, and: A poem is a small (or large) machine made of words. When I say there's nothing sentimental about a poem, I mean that there can be no part, as in any other machine, that is redundant.
>
> Prose may carry a load of ill-defined matter like a ship. But poetry is a machine which drives it, pruned to a perfect economy. As in all machines, its movement is intrinsic, undulant, a physical more than a literary character.[35]

A poem is an interior space, a room. In Williams's work, or Creeley's, or that of Emily Dickinson (who was a patron saint to them both), poems map the domestic space physically, as well as in the mind and emotions. A refined economy of words: a dance within the sphere.

If epic is a poem containing history, then lyric contains domesticity.

At Black Mountain, 'home' looked different than it had before. A new take on common living. An intensity we may all be hesitant to live in. *To open eyes.* To open eyes and make them see. What's often hardest to see is what we may reach out and touch. *Some secret touch.* Memory. And the poem. Some kind of coming home.

History is the tale of domestic interiors multiplied.

A physical more than a literary character.

I have lived the last several years in Stoneybatter. This small, autonomous village next to Dublin's city centre is one of the oldest parts of the city. Its streets still have Viking names. When I first moved to Stoneybatter, we lived in a tiny cottage on Sigurd Road. Sigurdson, my mother's maiden name, half-written on blue signs pointing me home.

She collapsed. Or slumped more like, in the way it was described to me later. She never regained consciousness or speech. For the sake of her story, she died that day, that minute, outside Paris, with a glass of champagne and music mixed with the sound of foreign ambulance shrieks and whistles. She died that day, if only dying were so simple.

What I've left out is the in-between. Those days between 1987 and today, in Dublin, where the story comes strangely into focus. When memory, played back like a quick shuffle of cue cards, skips through time, accumulating into fractured film stills, constituting a life.

In those stills, I find both beauty and brokenness. Often in the same form, shapes made from the unending push and pull of ego, insecurity, and silence. I had not spoken to my mother for several weeks when the phone rang. I took the call. At the other end, quiet for a moment. Then crying. Confusion. I knew then.

When I was young, there were days when I wished for something like this to happen. If only to be set apart, to be the one who has lost. To be, finally, lost. Who has not imagined his own death, or the death of someone close, and imagined it so that the crowd of mourners mourns for you, you alone and specifically? Only then do they recognise certain things in you, a hearty recklessness that sets you apart. In these imagined scenarios, you either watch as a ghost over your own funeral, looking down, feeling pity, pain, and pleasure all at once in the reactions of people gathered there. Or you imagine standing beside the grave as one is lowered down, your grief a singularizing enclosure out of which you may look at the world in detached, knowing silence.

But life and death are not so.

For ten days she hung on in intensive care. A brain detached from a body detached from a soul detached from the world.

To teach is the single act.

This machine must be unsentimental.

Poets are the Only Pedagogues

'I instruct not; I awake'
– Ezra Pound, 'Raphaelite Latin,' *Book News Monthly* (1906)

From the beginning, Black Mountain developed practice-based pedagogies that owed equally to American progressive education models and the Bauhaus influence brought by the Alberses and others. The only constant was experimentation. In the college's final phase – Charles Olson's Black Mountain – there was a marked turn toward poetics as pedagogy. In Olson's teaching, as well as Creeley's, William Carlos Williams and Ezra Pound sit at the heart of a useful, experimental movement in US poetry. Both Olson and Creeley corresponded with Pound and Williams. Each elder poet possessed a certain authority, as well as a determination in learning and teaching through poetry. Pound's publisher James Laughlin writes in *Pound as Wuz*,

> Pound was born a teacher, even if not destined to be a professor. He could not keep himself from teaching. In one way or another he was always teaching. The *Cantos* themselves are a kind of teaching. *Ut doceat, ut moveat, ut delectet.* They move us, they delight us, but above all they teach us.[36]

The dominant tone of Pound's poems – especially in *The Cantos* – is dogmatic and pedagogical. This has perhaps been taken for granted by his readers, as it took until 2012 to publish a book of essays, *Ezra Pound and Education* (ed. Yao & Coyle), that systematically addresses Pound's efforts to reform the world through his brand of education. His pedagogical program was hindered by disgraceful political views and confabulations later in his life, but Pound did succeed in passing on a distinctively pedagogical poetic approach to a younger generation of writers

– particularly those who were in direct correspondence with 'Ez,' like Olson and Creeley.

Ezra Pound and Charles Olson, Spoleto, 1965

Charles Olson Research Collection
Archives and Special Collections at the Thomas J. Dodd Research Center
University of Conecticut Libraries

Most plainly pedagogical of Pound's published works are his prose books, from *The Spirit of Romance* (1910) to – more importantly – his *ABC of Reading* (1934) and *Guide to Kulchur* (1938). They are presented as classroom materials, while his anthologies and translations point to methods of teaching and learning. During the period of these publications in the 1930s, Pound lived in Rapallo, where he presided as rector and sole faculty of his own 'Ezuversity,' described thus by Laughlin:

> Apparently convened at a dinner table, in the tradition of the nineteenth-century books of 'table-talk,' the Ezuversity never [. . .] went on holiday [. . .]. He lectured, sometimes hectored, conducted correspondences, and whenever possible conversed with just about anyone willing to listen. The name 'Ezuversity'

inevitably suggests a certain arrogance in the conviction that any one man could replace an entire faculty of
scholars and teachers [. . .]. But the name also suggests
an informality and even self-mockery.[37]

In Laughlin's description, Ezuversity 'courses' sound remarkably
like conditions at Black Mountain, particularly in the later days
of the desperately impoverished Olson period:

The Ezuversity was an ideal institution for a twentieth-century goliard. First of all, there was no tuition.
Ezra was always hard up, but he wouldn't take any payment. The only expenses I had were renting a room and
paying my meals with Mrs. Pound [. . .]. The classes
usually met at the lunch table. They might begin with
Ezra going through the day's mail, commenting on the
subjects that it raised.[38]

Olson was known to share bits of his voluminous correspondence with Creeley, Duncan, and others in his classes at Black
Mountain; Creeley called his correspondence with Olson a 'college of letters.' Before Creeley arrived at Black Mountain, his
work was well known there, despite the fact that he was not
published widely enough for more general recognition. Both
Olson and Creeley were engaged in their own letter writing
with Pound, who gave Creeley needed advice in establishing *The
Black Mountain Review*. After all, according to one of Pound's
most famous aphorisms from *ABC of Reading*, 'Literature is news
that stays news.' He required correspondents.

At the heart of Pound's pedagogy and his teaching practice in the Ezuversity was his rejection of institutional higher
learning in the United States, a rejection as bitter as that of
Black Mountain founder John Andrew Rice. Like Rice, Pound
maintained faith that the system could be changed by radical
revolution of literature and the arts; he never entirely gave up

on trying to change people's minds. As Pound's biographer, A. David Moody, points out, 'the only point in [Pound's criticism of the university] would be that he still held to an ideal of what a university ought to be. "Dead" though it might be, [. . .] it still stood for something in his mind.'[39]

Alan Golding asks, 'How do we explain Pound's ambivalent relationship with and ongoing address to pedagogical institutions?'

> To answer this question, we have to assume that Pound saw the academy as both audience and potential outlet or conduit for the cultural values he espoused [. . .] [and as] a site worth redeeming. This tendency is oddly Utopian, as if Pound cannot give up on some faith that universities can indeed play a crucial role in the transformation of culture.[40]

Black Mountain attempted the transformation of culture, and in some important ways it succeeded. In 1933, Rice envisioned a new kind of progressivism as antidote to decades of stodgy institutional learning. Pound's 1934 essay, 'The Teacher's Mission,' takes aim at the state of the profession in characteristically caustic terms. Yet it begins with an aphorism very much in tune with Black Mountain's position: 'The function of the teaching profession is to maintain the HEALTH OF THE NATIONAL MIND.'[41] BMC had been founded only one year earlier, and Rice would certainly have agreed, 'Education that does not bear on LIFE and on the most vital and immediate problems of the day is not education but merely suffocation and sabotage.'[42] The violence of the language – similar to Rice's advocacy for a humanizing education in the face of domestic and international catastrophe – is imbued with impending calamity: war, and the shape of 'the national mind' cannot be extricated. As the United States moved through the decades of the '30s and '40s, its people came up against the limitations of knowledge and conventional education in times of unprecedented horrors. Black Mountain thrived with a certain amount of chaos and uncertainty. Olson and Creeley emerged under the powerful influence of Ezra Pound, but in time their master had to be rejected.

Reviving Porter Sargent

In his 'Autobiography,' Creeley reveals a forgotten education theorist, integral to Pound's pedagogy, and avowedly central to Creeley's:

> It was my way of being serious – as I read Porter Sargent's extraordinary qualification of secondary private schools in America, sent me by Ezra Pound, who thought he'd be an active addition to the magazine I was trying to get started. His prefaces were bedrock judgments I still believe, and I wonder now if anyone remembers them, or Pound's interest. Certainly we recall John Kasper, and the rest.[43]

The 'prefaces' Creeley mentions are not Pound's, but Sargent's – in his time an influential writer, publisher, and education critic. These prefaces were the widely read forewords Sargent wrote for his *Handbook of Private Schools*, first appearing in 1915 and continuing into the 1940s. The prefaces were collected into the weighty volume, *Between Two Wars: The Failure of Education, 1920–1940*. This is the book that Creeley must be referring to.

It is significant that Pound was sharing selections, or possibly even the entire seven-hundred-plus-page book of Sargent's with Creeley, who himself seems bemused by the fact that nobody acknowledges this influence. (Though, as he writes bitingly, they certainly remember Pound's friendship with John Kasper, one of twentieth-century America's most virulent racists.)

In the Pound archive at his alma mater, Hamilton College, we find at least fourteen items labelled, 'Porter Sargent Materials Owned by Ezra Pound at St. Elizabeths Hospital; Gift of Omar Pound.' At the very top of the list is *Between Two Wars*, along with various reviews and articles on Sargent's book.

Between Two Wars is a detailed, year-by-year critique of

educational practices in the United States from 1920 to 1940. It draws a vivid picture of the pedagogical landscape in which Black Mountain was founded, and finds in the failures of general education the root causes of world wars and authoritarian misrule.

Sargent writes,

> The training of the young in awareness and understanding might have saved us from failure. But our faith in ancient precepts, adherence to traditions, and reliance on fetishes gave us confidence when fear should have warned us. When imminent crisis was upon us fear paralyzed instead of stimulating creative thought [. . .]. It soon became apparent that dictators in Italy, Germany, and Russia were using education to further their purposes. At closer view in England and America we were not aware of how the same process was going on.[44]

Pound paradoxically demanded we 'make it new' while constantly looking back, reviving ancient and medieval poetry and music in a revisionist tradition of his own. Porter Sargent, like Josef Albers, advocated a break with the past – what he calls the 'Dead Hand.' Sargent commands some of Pound's polemical vigour. In 'The Dead Hand' piece, written for the sixteenth edition of his *Handbook* in 1932, he continues,

> Education looks ahead in these times to prepare us for what is to come. But the hand of the past is always reaching out to hold us back. And it takes clear vision and bold leadership to break with the past, to step bravely into the unknown. The dead hand rests upon us and we think it duty, tradition, or religion [. . .].
>
> Where there's no strong faith or clear vision, tradition does much to furbish what might be barren lives.

> But with tradition, as with antiques, an increased
> demand leads to imitation and too high a price for the
> spurious.[45]

Pound's biographer A. David Moody suggests that, 'recalling
Schelling's declaration that "The University is not here for the
exceptional man," [Pound] concluded "the 'university' is dead."'[46]
To the poet, the university might very well have been dead. (At
least, the American university system was far away from his
concerns in Rapallo and his pupils at the Ezuversity.) Sargent's
critiques gave him powerful ammunition. But a movement was
taking place in the United States toward experimental, egalitarian education.

Sargent gives an authoritative history of 'progressive education' in *Between Two Wars*, arriving at the view that 'Education
in America is an inheritance, a survival, and a development. Like
ourselves, it comes from Europe, chiefly from England, with
strong and repeated influences from Germany.'[47] The English
public schools, says Sargent, aimed at making 'gentlemen,'
whereas in America – where they 'left it to Irish bosses' who
had not the 'distaste for the democratic machinery' – 'our educational institutions as a whole have had the ideal of making
"rugged individuals" and good citizens rather than gentlemen.'[48]
Yet the failure of this system, Sargent argues, led to the political,
economic, and cultural catastrophes of the twentieth century.
Without active reassessment and continual progress of our education systems, we are not immune to further sickness.

Sargent's influence on Black Mountain may not be as widely
recognized as that of John Dewey – whom Sargent calls 'the
most eminent living American philosopher who has had the
greatest influence on educational thought in America, Europe,
and Asia.' But he saw how Dewey's education philosophy remade
teaching and learning in the United States:

> Out of all application of the scientific method to

the processes of brain and mind has come a leavening influence. Interpreted and applied by Edward L. Thorndike it has given us the beginnings of a scientific method in education. Fused in the mind of John Dewey with ideals of democracy it has exerted a great and broadening influence. So the work of Dewey and Thorndike touches the subject of education at every point [. . .]. The informal, joyous, active, experimental school which is so largely the outgrowth of Dewey's stimulus and teaching seems a bedlam to the old-fashioned teacher. Just so our American democracy seems to the Prussian junker. Life is not so systematic and so ordered as the old time school discipline.[49]

I imagine so vividly Creeley reading these passages, passed on by Pound. There are echoes of Creeley's statement,

Coming of age in the forties, in the chaos of the Second World War, one felt the kinds of coherence that might have been fact of other time and place were no longer possible. There seemed no logic, so to speak, that could bring together all the violent disparities of that experience. The arts especially were shaken and the *picture of the world* that might previously have served had to be reformed.[50]

There are echoes, too, of both Pound's and Black Mountain's appeals to the scientific method, not just as metaphor, but also as practice. Sargent's monumental and sadly near-forgotten writing contextualizes US education during the period in which Black Mountain came to life. Pound was reading Sargent while incarcerated at St. Elizabeths, and he was sending Sargent's writing to Creeley. Sargent gives a vigorous critique of US education in the interwar period, and we know that he also sent his son – L. Porter Sargent – to study at Black Mountain College.

***

I came to Black Mountain through the poets who lived and taught there. Creeley first, then Olson, then, sometime later, Robert Duncan. I know now that the range of poetic sensibility was far greater than what is captured in Donald Allen's anthology, *The New American Poetry 1945–1960*, which first presented the 'Black Mountain Poets' to the reading public.

Many more people – students and teachers in all disciplines – wrote poems at Black Mountain, and many of the women – M. C. Richards, Hilda Morley – who wrote most seriously are left out of the picture, subsumed by the size of Olson's ambitions, or the later fame of Creeley and Duncan.

Josef Albers's speech above is a projective poem. He wrote his own remarkable verse, seen for example in his *Poems and Drawings* from 1958. At an early stage, still in Germany, Albers wrote verse-form letters to his best friend Franz Perdekamp.

He and many others ought to be considered Black Mountain poets.

The commonality is a sense of words as *material*. Poetics as craft and design. Language at its most fundamental. Vowels. And pigments. Olson saw the page as a canvas words dance over.

The Slow Westward Motion

> the generation of those facts
> which are my words, it is coming
>
> from all that I no longer am,
> yet am, the slow westward motion of
>
> more than I am
>
> Charles Olson, 'Maximus to Gloucester, Letter 27 [withheld]'

In the opening of his 'Fragments' for Ezra Pound, Charles Olson writes,

> I hate this anti-Semite! this revolutionary simpleton, as Yeats called him. [. . .] But for Christ sake have the courage to admit that Pound faced up to the questions of our time. I think he shows himself a traitor to more important things than the U.S. No man can attack a race and remain useful to anyone as an artist.[51]

Olson had begun a period of visits to his 'master' in 1946, while Pound was in St. Elizabeths psychiatric hospital in Washington, D.C., where he avoided conviction on grounds of mental infirmity for his hate-filled, damnable broadcasts on Rome radio during the Second World War. A great many writers, including Olson, came to Pound's defence, claiming that his contributions to the art of poetry outweighed his troubling on-air invective.

At the time he was visiting St. Elizabeths, Olson had not yet established himself as a poet. He still toiled in literary apprenticeship, approaching Pound as an artistic father he needed both to impress and replace. Pound's politics were particularly troubling to Olson, who had spent the previous years working for the

Foreign Language Division of the Office of War Information, the Democratic Party, and the Roosevelt campaign. Pound 'can talk all he likes about the *cultural lag* in America [. . .],' Olson writes, 'but he's got a 200 year *political lag* in himself.' Olson's political idealism, shaken by the Bomb and Truman's 'merchandise men,' flares again when confronted by Pound's reactionary pronouncements:

> It is not enough to call him a fascist.
>
> He is a fascist, the worst kind, the intellectual fascist, this filthy apologist and mouther of slogans which serve men of power. It was a shame upon all writers when this man of words, this succubus, sold his voice to the enemies of the people.

Olson finds Pound's betrayal of the Word more objectionable than the accusation of treason against the State. In opposition to these political stances, Olson finds the courage to match his own poetic powers (at this point little in evidence) against the overwhelming authority of his modernist master. Pound's *Cantos* became the standard against which Olson would measure himself. In their encounters at St. Elizabeths, there is a comical (literal) measuring: 'Then we got to the question of size. I figured he had a 36 waist. Which was my own: saying, you can't be bigger than me. He made as if to measure himself. No, not any bigger than you!'[52]

***

Charles Olson was born on December 27, 1910 in Worcester, Massachusetts. Son of a Swedish father and Irish mother, he towered over his parents at an early age. His most important childhood memories were of his father, a postman, walking his mail route, and of summers spent in a tiny house near the sea at Gloucester, the town on Cape Anne, Essex County, which Olson would place at the centre of his own epic sequence, *The Maximus Poems*.

Olson was a precocious student and a powerful debater. A prize for debating resulted in a trip around Europe, during which he met W. B. Yeats in Ireland. It would be many years before Olson would turn to poetry and imitate Yeats's voice in an address to Pound ('This is Yeats Speaking'), but his meeting with the great poet in 1928 stirred an early interest in poetic heritage. According to Tom Clark,

> [Yeats's] polite remarks about the lineage of the Hines clan [Olson's mother's relations] were sufficient to convince Charlie that his own mother's aunt must have been the same Mary Hines who had, according to Yeats, been 'the beloved of the blind poet Raftery and the most beautiful woman in all Western-Ireland.'[53]

Years later, when Creeley heard of his own family's Irish relations, he writes,

> my mother finally told me
> indeed the name Creeley was Irish –
>
> and the heavens opened, birds sang,
> and the trees and the ladies spoke
> with wondrous voices. The power of the glory
> of poetry – was at last mine.
>
> ('Theresa's Friends', from *Later*)

This fascination in both Olson and Creeley looks back to the bardic traditions of an ancient culture, wherein the poet served a more central function and higher purpose than his twentieth-century descendants. (As an American poet living in Ireland, they speak to me directly.) The betrayal of Pound occasioned a revision of the poet's place in the world, for he had made the strongest case for the poet's role in society, before bending to Hitler and Mussolini.

Sensing his own powers, Olson began to associate poetry with the powers of the physical body and the breath. If Pound's crimes were against the Word, Olson would hold the Word sacred by remaining 'one with [his] skin.'[54]

Yet it was in prose, and particularly in the work of Herman Melville, that Olson found his first authoritative literary interest. After distinguishing himself with a thesis on Melville at Wesleyan College, Olson entered Harvard as a PhD candidate in the famed American Studies program under F. O. Matthiessen. Olson's major contribution to Melville scholarship was the study of the nineteenth-century writer's personal library. Of particular interest were Melville's annotated copies of Shakespeare, which he was reading while at work on *Moby-Dick*. Olson managed to construct an original reading of Melville's masterpiece by paying close attention to its Shakespearean parallels. The resulting book published in 1947, *Call Me Ishmael*, which also made use of Olson's assiduous research into the US whaling economy and first-hand narratives of sailors and shipwrecks, is a masterpiece of literary criticism, written from the poet's perspective in the lineage of unconventional scholarship including D.H. Lawrence's *Studies in Classic American Literature* and William Carlos Williams's *In the American Grain*. In *Ishmael*, Olson declares, 'I take SPACE to be the central fact to man born in America, from Folsom Cave to now. I spell it large because it comes large here. Large, and without mercy.'[55]

Academic critics were puzzled by *Ishmael*. Yet it has become a major text, particularly for poets venturing into literary scholarship. In an essay on *Ishmael* – titled, 'Where Should the Commander Be?' – Susan Howe writes, 'A critic's dialogue with the thinking of writing should be a clarification and understanding that an author's major meanings are often unspoken. At the threshold of academicism and poetry – sympathy is passionate morality. *Call Me Ishmael* is SPACE in which Charles Olson, an outcast from the world of art in name only, integrates Melville into himself.[56] This integration is also my subject and preoccupation. Voices of the past project into our future. I find my meaning in the SPACE between.

From *Ishmael*, Olson moved further away from the academy and actively pursued the writing of poems. Early pieces, such as those collected in his first book of verse, *Y & X*, published by Black Sun Press in 1949, show his interest in the interactions of poetry and visual arts. The poems are responses to drawings by the Italian-American artist Corrado Cagli. Associations with visual artists and practitioners in other fields deepened when Olson arrived at Black Mountain College for the first time in 1948 as a visiting lecturer, on the invitation of Josef Albers.

In 1950, Creeley, who was still years away from his own Black Mountain period, started putting together a magazine that was never to be printed, *The Lititz Review*. However, much of the material he gathered ended up in Cid Corman's *Origin* magazine, a forerunner to Creeley's *The Black Mountain Review* and an important early outlet for Olson's poems. The poems Creeley received from Olson did not quite 'make it,' but upon reading Olson's staggering *Ishmael* and initiating a correspondence with its author, Creeley was stunned by the articulations he found there.

> In returning Olson's poems to Vincent [Ferrini], I made the somewhat glib remark that he seemed to be 'looking for a language,' and got thereby my first letter from Olson himself, not particularly pleased by my comment and wanting to discuss further, like they say. The letters thus resulting were really my education just that their range and articulation took me into terms of writing and many other areas indeed which I otherwise might never have entered.[57]

With these letters, and with *Ishmael*, Creeley realized the authority Olson possessed: 'I remember my own dumbfounded reception of that book – from a man I had assumed to be sharing my own position of unpublished hopefulness.'[58]

Whether or not Olson was still looking for a language, he was certainly looking for a livelihood. With the ascendance of Harry Truman, politics failed him, and Olson's general revulsion at the state of mainstream academia (including bitterness over *Ishmael*'s reception), made it difficult to imagine what kind of life could incorporate a rapidly developing poetic sense with the practical demands of a family, home, and career. Here his friend, the writer Edward Dahlberg, lent valuable support. Dahlberg had been teaching (very briefly) at Black Mountain College. (Initially, Dahlberg was thrilled by the college, but within two weeks he was decrying the 'murderous' landscape. He fled that very day and never returned.) On Dahlberg's recommendation, Albers invited Olson to the college. Despite his initial reluctance to teach, Olson recognized the college's potential to shape his life and work. Creeley recalls,

> One time at Black Mountain [Olson] said to me, 'I need a college to think with,' meaning, I understood, that he wanted the multiplicity of instance, all particular and active, not the discrete or isolating possibilities of a chosen few. 'Come into the world,' he said, 'Take a big bite.'[59]

Olson began to develop the *speculative expansiveness* that would define his teaching style, and – indeed – characterize the voracious, if chaotic, intelligence of *The Maximus Poems*.

With apprentices such as Edward Dorn, Jonathan Williams, John Wieners, Joel Oppenheimer, Michael Rumaker, Fielding Dawson, and others, eventually Olson became the centre of an alleged Black Mountain 'school' of poets. Those younger poets were in fact students and followers of Olson. However, there is very little to link their work together beside an active interest in one another's writing, a general sense of the poem as a *field of action*, in Olson's phrase, and of course the fact of the college itself. Some of the poets linked to Black Mountain, such as Denise Levertov, never even set foot at the college, and are associated with it through Allen's anthology and Creeley's *Review*. Like the commercially convenient appellation 'Beat Generation,' the artists associated with the supposed 'Black Mountain School' rejected the title. Olson did so most forcefully, in an interview from 1968,

> I think that whole 'Black Mountain Poet' thing is a lot of bullshit. I mean, actually, it was created by the editor, the famous editor of that anthology, Mr. Allen [. . .]. There are people, for example, poets, who just can't get us straight, because they think we form some sort of a what? A clique or a gang or something. And that there was a poetics? Boy, there was no poetics. It was Charlie Parker. Literally, it was Charlie Parker.[60]

Olson stayed on at Black Mountain until the very end, serving as the college's final rector and taking on the unenviable task of liquidating the institution in 1957. In the Olson archives at the University of Connecticut, boxes of material show that Olson was plagued by this heavy responsibility for the rest of his life. He had many unfulfilled plans to carry on the Black Mountain project as a 'college on wheels' or as a new institution in New York City or Venice, California. He remained hopeful about the poet's role in the wider community – the 'polis,' as he put it. In his mind, the poem was still capable of political agency.

Olson's most influential piece of writing is not a poem, but rather one of his many essays. Published in 1950, his essay on 'projective verse' argues for a breath-metred poetry that breaks with old modes (or, more accurately, returns to earlier poetics before print). This is opposed to the 'non-projective' or, as Olson writes, '"closed" verse, that verse which print bred and which is pretty much what we have had, in English & American, and have still got, despite the work of Pound & Williams.'[61]

Olson's essay, which went under heavy revision in correspondence with Creeley, was included in Allen's anthology. Williams went so far as to quote Olson's essay at length in his *Autobiography*, pointing to Olson's projective verse as a breakthrough in thinking on poetic form. Williams's *Paterson*, which first started appearing in 1946, was of great interest to poets at Black Mountain. It gave a useful alternative to Pound's vision in *The Cantos*. Unlike Pound, Williams had remained in America, refusing exile. Williams used the common material of everyday life to craft poems as economical machines. His *Paterson* is a documentary epic that contains local history, and he maintained his belief in American democracy, while Pound flatly rejected it. However, like Pound, Williams struggled to find a poetic form that would make his vision cohere.

Williams's approach to writing was shaped by the painters and other artists he encountered, from Marcel Duchamp to his friend Charles Demuth. At Black Mountain, vital interactions between the disciplines of painting and writing were demonstrated again and again, from Albers to Olson, Kline to Dawson, Dan Rice to Creeley. Olson's poetics echo the interdisciplinary nature of studies at Black Mountain, from the 'action painters' associated with the college, to dancers Merce Cunningham and Katherine Litz, who showed Olson the true possibilities of a poetics of *motion*. Black Mountain relentlessly broke down boundaries between disciplines in art and learning. It did so consciously, but also as a matter of practical fact. The tiny, remote college – hardly ever housing more than a few dozen teachers and students at once – had none of these boundaries by virtue of its size and the close proximity of its inhabitants. Cunningham and Buckminster Fuller found intellectual affinities at Black

Mountain in the most unremarkable circumstances: coffee and breakfast in the dining hall at Lake Eden. Whereas most of our universities erect impassable boundaries keeping disciplines apart, Black Mountain encouraged the same kind of intuitive expansiveness characteristic of Olson's interests. While at Black Mountain, Olson initiated collaborations in theatre, dance, drawing, and painting. His great work *Apollonius of Tyana* was written at Black Mountain as a dance-verse-drama. Olson's interest in Mayan glyphs – associated with his travels documented in *Mayan Letters* (published by Creeley's Divers Press) – were shared by artists at Black Mountain including Ben Shahn and Katherine Litz, both of whom participated in a 'glyph exchange' with Olson at the college. As casual as some of these interactions could be at Black Mountain, they had profound effects on participants in the community. After the college's closing, they took them out into the wider world and incorporated them into their practice and teaching for decades.

Olson's *college to think with* was a living organism, laying out (like a 'glass slide,' as he proposed) the individual for examination. While Olson held court and controlled things through his domineering personality, he also gained poetic and pedagogical strength from the interaction of many arts and disciplines in the same highly charged atmosphere.

I have pointed to a number of education theorists and practitioners who influenced teaching at Black Mountain College: John Dewey, John Andrew Rice, and Porter Sargent, as well as the poetic pedagogies of Pound and Williams and the Bauhaus fundamentals of Albers, Gropius, and Itten. This constellation of important education thinkers goes beyond the idea of Black Mountain as simply a 'progressive' college; the sense of poetry and poetics as pedagogical stances in their own right developed in the Olson era, if not by total design then by characteristic and relentless experimentation. To this distinguished list of teachers and theorists must be added the British logician Alfred North

Whitehead, whose book *The Aims of Education* was first published in 1932, placing it within the context of Black Mountain's departure from conventional modes in education.

Olson's borrowings from Whitehead have been pointed out by many critics, George Butterick chief among them in his *Guide to The Maximus Poems*. For example, Olson's great 'Letter 27 [withheld],' a poem I draw on regularly, seems to have been 'withheld' from *Maximus* precisely because it borrows so directly from Whitehead's *Process and Reality*. But it is Whitehead's *The Aims of Education* that I point to for a clearer view of pedagogical thought and practice at Olson's Black Mountain. Along with *Process and Reality, Aims* was the only other book by Whitehead found in Olson's personal library (reconstructed by Ralph Maud, and now housed at the University of Connecticut.)

Whitehead's essays on education channel his process philosophy, and we find echoes in both practice and pedagogy at Black Mountain. The arguments fueling experimentation at the college, coalescing in the early 1930s and developing into the '40s and '50s, are articulated in simple and provocative terms. Whitehead's first determination is the activity of education against 'inert ideas': 'In training a child to activity of thought, above all things we must be aware of what I will call "inert ideas" – that is to say, ideas that are merely received into the mind without being utilised, or tested, or thrown into fresh combination.'[62] This statement brings us back to Rice's idea of the student's activity 'amid the facts' being more important than 'the facts themselves,' and also to Olson's insistence on the 'USE' of the projective poem, the kinetic activity of words and poetic form.

In his 'Bibliography on America for Ed Dorn,' written for his favoured Black Mountain disciple, Olson demands the 'saturation job,' delving deep into one subject, rather than the scattered approach of other, less disciplined methodologies. Whitehead argues the very same: 'Let us now ask how in our system of education we are to guard against this mental dryrot [. . .]. "Do not teach too many subjects," and again, "What you teach,

teach thoroughly.'"[63] Black Mountain's pared-down curriculum, limited by necessity, fit this model. Whitehead also argues for the constant active use of the mind from the very beginning of education. There is no preliminary to this method; it happens from the start. He takes issue with the theory that 'runs thus: The mind is an instrument, you first sharpen it, and then use it [. . .].'

> I do not know who was first responsible for this anology of the mind to a dead instrument [. . .]. I have no hesitation denouncing it as one of the most fatal, erroneous, and dangerous conceptions ever introduced into the theory of education. The mind is never passive; it is a perpetual activity, delicate, receptive, responsive to stimulus. You cannot postpone its life until you have sharpened it.[64]

Olson teaching at Black Mountain
Courtesy of the Western Regional Archives, State Archives of North Carolina

In Olson's pedagogy, the active mind was to be trained through two disciplines in particular: mythology and archaeology. Based on Albers' summer arts institutes at the college, in 1953 Olson devised an institute dedicated to what he called the 'New Sciences of Man.' Later, he writes in 'A DRAFT OF A PLAN FOR THE COLLEGE' at Black Mountain in 1956, archaeology is the method, where the mythological is the matter. It was archeology, indeed, which broke loose the birth of new knowledge around 1875, it was the digging up of the past not the mere recording or repeating the history of it. It was the objectification, the literal seeking and finding of *the objects* of the past of man which took down all generalization with it [. . .]. And you can't do that by simply sitting around in wonder and fantasy and trouble over what happens to one or what one dreams. You have to have the experience of hard objects, of panning, of what does wash out when all the water is out of it. And archeology has this vivid reality of its own practice, decisively, now, more than the experimental method of old science [. . .]. Thus, how it is we, at Black Mountain, insist upon a knowledge of the archeological until a method of viewing anything as to be dug out, is a habit. It is not an easy habit to turn one self into.[65]

The volume containing all of Olson's poems he deemed strong enough for posterity, beside *The Maximus Poems*, is titled *The Archaeologist of Morning*. As with Pound, making things new called for reassessing old processes. The poetry of 'post-modern' man – of man in the twentieth and twenty-first centuries – would be as active and ranging as the history uncovered in exhumed cities. It would constitute entire lives, whole civilizations, canons of knowledge and art. Olson's ambitions were ultimately tragic in their grandeur, yet his writing is often heroic in its accomplishment.

One can imagine how Olson's views – and his manner – ran counter to the established writing and teaching of his time. Since his Harvard days, he harboured animosity for academia, and the critics were not often kind in return. Despite the undeniable impact he had on a generation of poets – an influence perpetuated by Creeley, Howe, and others after Olson's death in 1970 – academia has shied away from his towering body of work. Harsh criticisms, some fair and some not, have been levelled. Olson has been called homophobic, despite his close relationships to gay writers, such as Black Mountain students John Wieners and Michael Rumaker. (Along with artistic freedoms, Black Mountain was – for some – remarkably tolerant of sexual preferences.) Olson's condescension to women has been a persistent complaint, no doubt harming his reputation from the 1970s onward, when feminist literary theory was ascendant, particularly in the academy. Olson's attitudes toward women cannot be excused off-hand, and we puzzle at the fact that women – like Frances Boldereff, in her brilliant correspondence with Olson – were essential to his artistic development. Still, in the breadth of his interests and the sweep of his vision, Olson has much to give to writers and readers in our twenty-first century.

A book of essays, *Contemporary Olson* (2015), edited by poet and critic David Herd, takes on the problematic reception of Olson's work and tries to assess what Olson may mean today. In his introduction, Herd points to one of Olson's most influential achievements, his new ways of conceiving and executing the form of the poem:

> By the way Olson indents, centres, left and right aligns, by the way he uses the typewriter to open the poetic page up to the kind of dynamics one associates with painting, he disrupts the tendency to simply read the poem straight through [. . .].
>
> The way Olson uses the page to produce a field of inter-related elements, thereby calling for a reading that cuts back and forth across space and time, is undoubtedly fundamental to his poetic practice. It should also be understood, however, to be of the order of a visual clue. What we are asked to understand is the

way that visuality figures relations, especially human relations, how the reciprocity and interference of feedback inform both human agency and historical change.

Howe makes a similar argument in 'Where Should the Commander Be?': 'The spatial expressiveness of much of Olson's writing is seldom emphasized enough. It is evident here [in *Call Me Ishmael*] even on the page of Contents. This feeling for seeing in a poem, is Olson's innovation.' Olson's formal inventions and experiments are not alienating *postmodernisms*; they are attempts to access a human agency, to bring alive in the poem our fundamental human interactions. Breaking up the line in the way Olson does, and even breaking up the text so that the reader must move back and forth across the page and through the poem, these become common in poetry after 1950. (They also point away from Olson's projective verse and toward a different sense of his achievement as primarily a visual poet.) The elements in Olson's writing that can be impenetrable are the sweeping historical referents and unexplained allusions. Yet the personal view, the position of the poet within history, within the *polis*, situates these difficulties in what Olson calls the 'Human Universe.'

Herd helpfully points out that, for Olson,

the view was a significant category, dealt with at length in the series of seminars delivered at Black Mountain College in 1956 (the transcriptions of which were subsequently published as *The Special View of History*). [. . .] The purpose of Olson's seminars was to gain an understanding of the concept of human view, to grasp the historical and geographical forces that combine to shape it. Crucially, though, the view is *a* view, its definition and limitation being precisely what makes it one among many. When, at the beginning of his poem, Olson presents Maximus, 'Off-shore, by islands,' what he is precisely presenting is a view, a strictly limited perspective. One could contrast the opening of *The Cantos*, which gives us no view. In Olson, authority is questioned from the outset.[66]

An authority such as Pound's is disempowered in the human view from Olson's side of the mid-century divide. Pound's failure to 'cohere' *The Cantos* – as he famously remarked – is perhaps a failure of vision. Olson's own sprawling mess of a masterpiece fails at times to cohere, while his epic's ambition is similar to Pound's in its record of a poet's thought developing over decades in a poem that activates history. But it is important to look at Olson's turn away from Pound and toward the more democratic Williams, the 'clean animal' who stayed behind in the United States and wrote in the American vernacular. *Paterson* is much like Olson's Gloucester sequence in that it centres on the topography and local history of a common American town. As a young man, during summers at Gloucester, Olson worked in the post office as a mail carrier, just like his father. After Black Mountain (by way of Buffalo) he returned there. His point of view is that of the postman, an ambulatory, objective view of life in an ordinary place. In a local sense, akin to James Joyce's Dublin, Olson's everyday Gloucester is elevated to the heroic and mythological.

Despite their fundamental divergence, Olson admired the way Pound 'faced up to the questions of [his] time.' Olson's work veers from direct political and pedagogical statements to complex mythopoetics. Yet his approach – his curiosity and critical inquiry – may continue to inform our own intellectual and artistic searching. Olson's work interrogates the ways in which scholarship and the arts interact. His teaching at Black Mountain underscores the need for disciplines to overlap, without segregating fields of knowledge and willing a kind of specialized ignorance. The saturation job is wide-ranging. His own interests were not contained to a single field. Rather, he depended on interactions within the kinetic field of the poem, the page, and the voice. There is in Olson a deep humanity and a relentless grasping for an art that contains our fragile and wondrous imagination:

Eyes,
& polis,
fishermen,
& poets
             or in every human head I've known is
             busy
both:
the attention, and
care
             however much each of us
             chooses our own
             kin and
             concentration[67]

Thoughts, in motion, on Black Mountain's *IMPLIED CENTRE*: Olson and the vortex of his achievement. A poetic responsibility: to hold at once opposing views, our Negative Capability. Maximus, the giant – the great accumulator. Hunting among stones and the monuments we build, to remember.

Charles Olson at Black Mountain College, by Jonathan Williams
Jonathan Williams Photographs
Yale Collection of American Literature
Beinecke Rare Book and Manuscript Library Yale University

Charles Olson at Black Mountain College, by Jonathan Williams

Jonathan Williams Photographs
Yale Collection of American Literature
Beinecke Rare Book and Manuscript Library Yale University

The Active Nucleus

Four years before they ever met at Black Mountain College, Olson and Creeley began their voluminous correspondence. The greatest of Olson's editors and exegetes, George F. Butterick, has written that 'the early letters, especially – and certainly those through 1954 [that is, leading up to Creeley's arrival at Black Mountain] – stand together as a critical document for understanding the emerging poetics of a generation, as well as, perhaps, of the poetries yet to come.' In the early letters, Butterick continues, 'they are working out a place for themselves at the frontiers of world writing, cut off by indifference and entrenched interests, seeking to communicate from their respective foxholes.' Olson and Creeley shared the active, sometimes conflicted, influences of Pound and Williams, and through their letters they began to work out what these conflicts and affinities might mean. Black Mountain resonates in Butterick's summation that 'at times it seems they wrote not to entertain, or even instruct, but to survive.'[68] The college too had to fight for survival, and Olson planned a venture that he hoped would ensure its continuation: *The Black Mountain Review*, edited in seven issues from 1954–1957.

Robert Creeley as a Spanish Assassin, by Jonathan Williams
Jonathan Williams Photographs
Yale Collection of American Literature
Beinecke Rare Book and Manuscript Library Yale University

In 1954, Olson invited Creeley to Black Mountain to teach and
to edit the proposed magazine, intended as a means of publiciz-
ing the dwindling college. Creeley, who was only twenty-eight
and had never taught before, had already made a number of
contacts as an editor, including his correspondences with Pound,
Williams, and Cid Corman. After Creeley's first attempt to
found a magazine – *The Lititz Review*, in 1950 – failed to get
off the ground, much of that material ended up in Corman's
era-defining *Origin* magazine, which first appeared in spring of

1951. Later on, Creeley would draw on poets featured in *Origin* for the core contributions *to The Black Mountain Review*.

Duberman notes that the poets collected in *Origin* and later *The Black Mountain Review* were 'in rebellion against the modalities then dominant in poetry and criticism, [and] had few outlets [for publishing their work].'[69] This points to both the circumstances of many of these poets – like Blackburn, Duncan, and Olson – who received scant positive critical reception from the poetry establishment, and also to what the *Review* wished to create as '"an active, ranging" section for critical writing that would be "prospective" – "would break down habits of 'subject' and gain a new experience of context generally."'[70]

The *Review*'s first four volumes bear covers designed by Japanese artist and poet Katue Kitasono, who was introduced to Creeley by Pound. The images are nearly identical, in triangular geometric shapes spilling down the page. We are reminded, perhaps, of the geometrical shapes of colour that emerge from a Josef Albers canvas. (It should be noted that both Dan Rice and Michael Rumaker hated the covers, and they complained to Creeley, who took action.) With volume five, which featured a cover by Los Angeles artist John Altoon, a friend of Creeley's who had been introduced by Black Mountain student Fielding Dawson, the magazine moves toward a more 'active', non-geometrical design.[71]

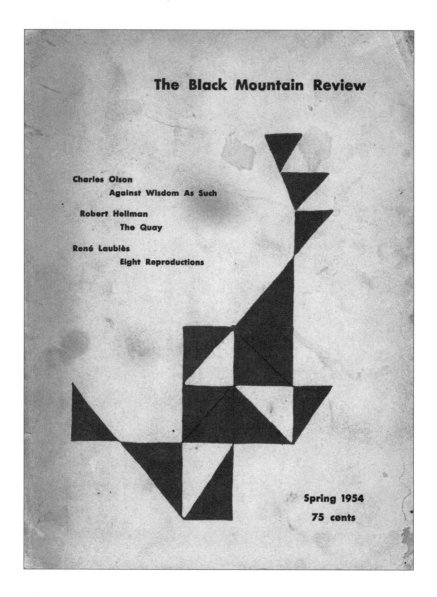

BMR 1 – Cover designed by Katue Kitasono (1954)
Archives and Special Collections at the Thomas J. Dodd Research Center
University of Connecticut Libraries

BMR 5 – Cover designed by John Altoon (1955)

Archives and Special Collections at the Thomas J. Dodd Research Center
University of Connecticut Libraries

Issue six sees a cover designed by Black Mountain artist Dan Rice. It is minimalist and suggestive of the 'open field' poetics of Olson and Duncan. This issue features Louis Zukofsky's essay on Shakespeare – 'Bottom: On Shakespeare – Part Two' – along with the work of a representative group of poets, including Duncan, Creeley, Levertov, Hilda Morley, Lorine Niedecker, and Olson. (Notice the higher female-to-male ratio than might be expected from the male-dominated Black Mountain scene.) Duncan's partner Jess Collins contributed some of his collage works, familiar to the Bay Area art scene of the '40s and '50s, which were featured on the covers of many of Duncan's books.

BMR 6 – Cover designed by Dan Rice (1956)

Archives and Special Collections at the Thomas J. Dodd Research Center
University of Connecticut Libraries

The Edward Corbett-designed seventh issue expanded the reach and editorial scope of *The Black Mountain Review*, with Allen Ginsberg as co-editor, alongside Creeley. It published works by many of Ginsberg's Beat Generation cohort in San Francisco and New York, including Jack Kerouac and William Burroughs, and printed Ginsberg's poem 'America.' This was the only issue not printed in Majorca, where Creeley had set up his Divers Press and where printing costs were comparatively cheap. It was instead printed by poet, photographer, and Black Mountain student Jonathan Williams, whose own Jargon Press published important works of the era revolving primarily around Black Mountain College, including Olson's *The Maximus Poems 1-10* in 1953.

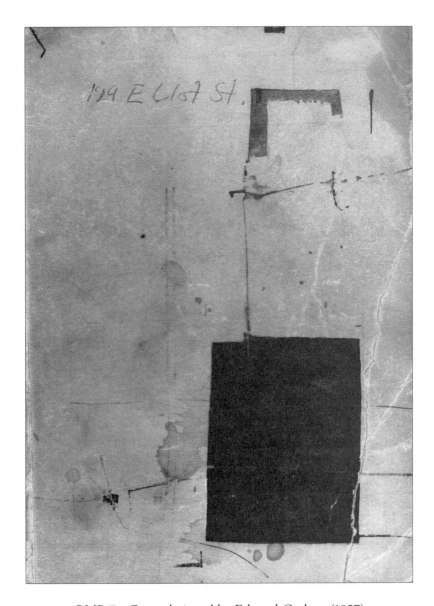

BMR 7 – Cover designed by Edward Corbett (1957)

Archives and Special Collections at the Thomas J. Dodd Research Center
University of Connecticut Libraries

. . . I had found excuse to write to both Ezra Pound and William Carlos Williams. I didn't know what I really wanted of them but was of course deeply honored that they took me in any sense seriously. Pound very quickly seized on the possibility of our magazine's becoming in some sense a feeder for his own commitments, but was clearly a little questioning of our *modus operandi*. What he did give me, with quick generosity and clarity, was a kind of *rule book* for the editing of any magazine. For example, he suggested I think of the magazine as a center around which, 'not a box within which/ any item.' He proposed that verse consisted of a constant and a variant, and then told me to think from that to the context of a magazine. He suggested I get at least four others, on whom I could depend unequivocally for material, and to make their work the mainstay of the magazine's form. But then, he said, let the rest of it, roughly half, be as various and hogwild as possible, 'so that any idiot thinks he has a chance of getting in.' [. . .] Williams in like sense gave us active support and tried to put us in touch with other young writers, as Pound also did, who might help us find a company.

– Creeley on *The Lititz Review*

Therefore there had to be both a press and a magazine absolutely specific to one's own commitments and possibilities. Nothing short of that was good enough.

– Creeley, 'Black Mountain Review'
from *Was That a Real Poem?*

Listening to Robert Creeley

A new language itself is heard. The poem is contained. The voice wound tight and restless. Bebop agility blows, following a suggested rhythm. An ability with emotion (as abstracted object). A young, sure voice, removed from home – from himself – set aside, imagined *revisioning.*

Robert Creeley's teaching became a vessel for his friends' speaking.

A generosity. An inability. A fact of human form. These are *machines.* Small or large.

And something automatic. A poem-a-day. Poems for night, too. The darkness surrounds us.

There are evenings alone – in Dublin, Berlin, New York, Paris – when Creeley speaks to a primary cause. *The hunt & the cause* (as I once misheard). 'Prime' in the *primitive.* These are our definitions. Something beyond circumference. Some enactment of the rights we claim as people and the speakers of the *poem.* Yet some forms fail. Some trail off and are eliminated. A few stay, *maintain.* You find such subtle variation.

Wake on this cold stone. The hours have been excavated and laid bare for exhibition. Your place, Creeley, was in *coming together.* Not obscure quotation but friendly invitation.

A syncopation of more than words. At times, of less.

A Poem (for R.C.)

> I work toward
> an acceptable structure
>
> of reality—
> a view that history
>
> takes shape as
> a column of air
>
> the poet (and poem)
> passes through

***

'Bach & Bird & Williams,' all you need – so Creeley says.

He came to music through a few futile years at the violin, and a college roommate whose record collection introduced him to the jazz of the thirties and forties.

At Black Mountain, Creeley met Dan Rice. They lived together and shared meagre provisions. Like twins: visual dance with words, in tune – in TIME.

SPACE of endless sea. And the mountain: phenomenology of poetic particulars.

Robert Creeley (left) and Dan Rice and Black Mountain,
by Jonathan Williams

Jonathan Williams Photographs
Yale Collection of American Literature
Beinecke Rare Book and Manuscript Library Yale University

Dan Rice was born one month after Creeley in the summer of 1926. He grew up in Long Beach, Southern California, thirty miles from where I was raised in Los Angeles. Rice was an accomplished trumpet player. In the early 1940s, he played with jazz greats Benny Goodman, Artie Shaw, and Stan Kenton.

Growing up in Los Angeles, I was initiated early into the Southern California jazz scene. At fourteen, I began studying with my mentor Peter Erskine, whose approach to music and life had a profound influence on me. He had met and played with Kenton for the first time when he was seven years old. In 1972, Peter took up his first professional gig with Kenton's jazz orchestra. The rest is history, as they say.

During the Second World War, Rice served in the Navy, one of many Black Mountain students who served or later attended the college under the GI Bill. The draft was a constant and worrying reality in the forties and fifties.

The GI Bill brought my father to college, first in his family. His schooling brought him to California.

As Creeley remembers, Rice 'spent over two years on a converted LSM, used as a rocket launcher – with some 70 men on board, never once in that time touching ground.' The SPACE of the sea is profound, opening up possibility 360 degrees round.

After graduating high school, I went straight to CalArts to study music in the jazz program directed by Charlie Haden. I continued study with Peter, and in whatever spare time I could find between rehearsals and gigs, I read deeply into the works of W. B. Yeats and James Joyce. Their world – their Dublin – seemed so far yet familiar. A grey and wasted counterpoint to the sun-drenched Southern California of which I had grown resentful and bored. I sensed possibility outside the United States. The music never left me; it is stronger in me today than it was in those days. But the world opened and an Irish landscape called me away. 'If you wanted to succeed, you had to go away.'

Rice eventually decided that he wanted to be more than a jazz musician; he was determined to become a composer. Music

had been transformed in the early decades of the twentieth century, particularly in Europe, and Black Mountain had bene-
fited, again, from composers and musicians fleeing to the United
States. Like those refugees from the Bauhaus, an influx of émi-
grés escaping war-torn Europe changed the musical shape of the
United States. Rice went to Black Mountain in order to study
composition under one such master, Heinrich Jalowetz, who
had been a protégé of Arnold Schoenberg and a core member
of the Second Viennese School of composers, along with Berg,
Webern, and Loos. Emigrating around the same time as many of
the Bauhaus artists in 1938, Jalowetz arrived at Black Mountain
and quickly became one of the college's most beloved teachers.
Along with Albers and Schawinsky, Jalowetz had an Old World
style and rigour that enhanced the experimental preoccupations
of the college, giving a much-needed framework for what could
otherwise be entirely free improvisations. In the Black Mountain
College Newsletter, Number 16, from November 1941, Jalowetz
was quoted from a speech he had given to the college faculty:

> We must differentiate between ideologies and ideas.
> Ideologies are always strictly excluding, asserting them-
> selves but discrediting any different opinion and put-
> ting anathemas on others. Our community must have
> a common idea; it must be based on ideas rather than
> on ideologies.
>
> Our college must give equal evaluation to all fields
> and take all of them extremely seriously, for only in
> this way can we reach a new kind of universality, an
> educational background which is opposed to the nar-
> row-minded specialised training that is a characteristic
> of average education today. This genuine universality
> can only be reached if everybody sees the whole world
> in his own field.
>
> We must avoid making a cult of words. Reliance on
> word magic makes it impossible to develop the genuine

universality that we can reach only if we do not indulge too much in general pronouncements. We must substitute actions for talking; we must make sure that what we say really means something.

(The same newsletter printed a notice of the most profound death in the community, that of nine-year-old Mark Dreier, killed in an automobile accident on October 8, 1941 near Lake Eden. On one of my visits to the Lake Eden campus, Ted Dreier, Jr., who had grown up at Black Mountain and studied there, remembered his brother's death while we walked up the path through the trees into the wooded area above the lake. We were quiet in the presence of this heavy loss, unrelieved after almost seventy-five years.)

The only thing grief has taught me...

When Dan Rice arrived at Lake Eden in 1946, he found that Jalowetz had just passed away. Sensing immediately that the community was unique in its approach to learning and living, he decided to stay on anyway.

Like many others at Black Mountain, Rice's encounters with Josef Albers changed the trajectory of his creative life. Rice said later, 'Anybody that touched Albers never got over it.' After a brief return to California to study architecture at Berkeley, Rice came back to Black Mountain, determined this time to become a painter.

Over ten years, Rice was one of the central figures at the college. He was important to Black Mountain's building program, taking a lead role in the construction of three of the college's buildings. His work as a painter is not as widely known as that of others in the Black Mountain orbit, like Franz Kline, Robert Rauschenberg, Robert Motherwell, Kenneth Noland, or Willem de Kooning. But Rice's abstract canvases are every bit as remarkable, composed with a delicate, precise energy. His canvases are *fields*, as Olson would have said. Their kinetic activity is just as lively today.

In an exhibition catalogue, *Dan Rice at Black Mountain College: Painter Among the Poets* (2014), Brian Butler sketches the important relationship that developed between Rice and Creeley, who was also deeply devoted to jazz music.[72] Both artists were interested in the ways they could adapt the rhythms, syncopations, and spacing of bebop into their own practices in different media. Olson held Rice in high regard, and on a number of occasions referred to Rice as the greatest living American painter. Some of Creeley's best early poems appear in the Black Mountain book collaboration with Rice, *All That Is Lovely In Men* (1955), published by Jargon Press.

During a building project at Lake Eden, an unwitting student gathered stones from the surrounding woods. One of those was the unmarked headstone on Heinrich Jalowetz's grave. It was incorporated into the wall of a new building and only discovered when the project was finished. Jalowetz's wife, Johanna – another beloved figure at the college – is said to have taken the mishap rather well. She was a kind woman just as her husband had been a kind and generous man. The physical plant of Black Mountain College is quite literally built on and around the remains of community members. Their spirits still haunt the grounds.

I have never visited my mother's grave. Her urn was not present at the funeral service. I write a form of inscription, where memory is false and facts fading. We *kneel to intellect*, to some purpose presupposed. For an active image, a coherence of skin and bone, life and love, music and material. Mostly, it is the SOUND that I remember.

Robert Creeley[73]

During the late '40s I'd come into contact with Charles Olson. Never in person, as it happens, but rather through correspondence. Started by my having been in touch with Vincent Ferrini in Gloucester through Cid Corman. Subsequently, again in the late '40s, Ferrini sent me some poems of Olson's as possible material for a magazine I was beginning to edit, or trying to edit, which finally became included in the first issue of *Origin* for the most part.

In any case, this led to a very active correspondence with Olson himself. So that relationship was continuing in that fashion from the late '40s to the time I went to Black Mountain in 1954. I went primarily on Olson's invitation, with the agreement of the then-existing faculty.

I was there as a teacher. I had been brought in to work in the writing program with Olson. And I subsequently had to do with students qualifying for graduation, such as Edward Dorn. The degree, which is noted for me as 'BA from Black Mountain,' is a bit euphemistic in this sense. When living in New Mexico a few years later, I was teaching at a day school for boys in Albuquerque. Because I literally had no degree – I left Harvard previous to getting one – I found myself in the awkward situation of having, ostensibly, no academic background.

I was trying then to get admitted to the graduate school. I needed some sort of qualifying degree from a college. I couldn't get it from Harvard, as it happened, so I was writing Olson of the dilemma. And he said, 'Well let me just give you one. I still exercise that authority.' Although the college had by that time closed. 'Let me give you a degree, simply that you were actually, say, three credits short of one, you obviously taught at Black Mountain. Let's assume that you could pass the courses you taught.' That was how the BA came to be. But I was never actually at Black Mountain as a student.

***

I should note, I think, that my first wife had gone to Black Mountain briefly as a student in the '40s. About '44. Having gone first to Radcliffe for a year, not liking that and looking around for an alternate school. She ended up in Black Mountain for a very short time indeed. While she was there, it was just before I went into the National Field Service, I managed to get down. This is before we were married. And so I spent two or three days there visiting her. At the time I remember that Alfred Kazan was on the faculty.

So I had a sense of the physical place. It was rather vague. By the time I returned, it was ten years later.

***

First impressions of the place as an actually physical plant were, from my point of view, very pleasant. It was highly informal. There seemed to be an intrinsic privacy permitted and encouraged. There were few students. I think that made an impression upon me, the fact that it was clearly having difficulty getting sufficient numbers of students. I don't think there could have been more than, say, twenty-five on my arrival.

I have a very vivid memory – this is my first meeting with Olson actually. I'd come back from Majorca, or rather I'd come from Majorca, stopped briefly in New York to see Paul Blackburn. I walked into the college in the very early morning. And I remember locating Olson's place and knocking on the door, and suddenly being confronted by Olson wearing a towel, otherwise naked. This very large man indeed saying, 'Come in, come in.'

I was very tentative about teaching. Well, personal circumstances were pretty hopeless at that time. My wife and I were just about – well, we hadn't come consciously to decide to separate, but we were obviously headed that way. I was very confused. I also literally never had a job of any active order, of any order. Since the time of marriage I had been dependent on a small income my wife had to manage my own way. This was a large step for me indeed, this job. And I came into it with a great deal of tentativeness. I remember my wife sending me a cable saying, 'If you just can't do it, by all means simply come back.'

So I spoke at that time even more lowly than I now do. I tended to mumble. Mike Rumaker years after said that the first three weeks of my teaching there no one, literally, in the class could hear me. And we finally ended up in a room so small, about six of us in this group. We ended up literally with our knees touching because otherwise it seemed I couldn't be heard.

Olson sort of swept me right along. We'd had this long correspondence, so we certainly were very familiar with each other's ways of thinking. But I can remember him saying – we had some breakfast, relaxed, and talked for a while – then he said, 'Well, are you ready to go?' And I thought, I'd like to wait a day or two . . . But he said, 'No, everybody's waiting so why don't you just start your first class this afternoon.' I said, the evening would probably be better. So, if I remember correctly, I started teaching on the day of my arrival at something like seven in the evening.

He very usefully got me into it before I had a chance to worry further.

So first impressions were of a fairly sparse circumstance, in a very lovely and open situation of place. With a variety of people, as I then came to know them. Dan Rice I had a brief correspondence with. He was there then as a kind of resident painter, partly student and partly simply resident. Joe Fiore was teaching painting. The other faculty I found very agreeable.

There was a kind of almost useful desperation to things that gave people a more active context. At least they had to think, and to come up with some sort of possibility, as they could . . .

Yours for a Call to Arms . . .

June 17, 1954

dear Olson / I am driven by the need for correspondences to make (or attempt) for the first time a primitive allotment of the day – with its period (the early morning) for letters; it (the need) is backlog piling up, pushing against some months now. I had returned to typing – money pleasures [pressures?] America's own version of the slave camp; and for a year have suffered under + in the self-destructive stop-drama. Today then (June 17) I have rudely disrupted that course – and the jam of logs is shifting (nerves shifting, [. . .] for the current of speech).

Thus – to make my beginning. John Adams writes 'I will rouse up my mind and fix my attention.' And had that task of arousing himself to do, with a rigor, before he find himself. In your *PROJECTIVE VERSE* – the drive toward a maximum energy – an exertion in the works of it, measured phrases to drive, the engine designed wise movement: instructive each time at a level vital within 'what yare saying.'

Writing the letter to you about your work and then seeing it again, as you suggested it, to be printed, I thought of it in the context I was sure of a critical response to the Maximus Letters. Now 'they' must go back, it ran, to sum up, to sit up, to set up their guns. All for or against this. But we see now that the current runs underground; it does not decrease the excitement that these signs of new (re-newed) life in the language to not appear (tho be thrust in the faces of) upon the surfaces of this literary world of not-critical criticism.

All the academy that despised here my ardent consultation of *The Cantos* (as a breaking up into movement of the old log-piles) now address themselves to sorting, identifying, deifying the old log piles to spite the energy set there about to break it up.

Only Stein remains freshly disrepute-full. And the 'objectivists,' 'dadaists' and 'surrealists' (of the absolute order – Breton, Tzara, Magritte, Peret) indigestible to the professional readers. They demand 'the unique presence,' the actuality: beyond / before the 'image' – I don't have right at hand the files of *Origin* but someplace thereabouts you bolstered up my growing adherence to thingness. This is a box with nothing inside but the inside inside. All the Pandora's woes and hopes – the glamours – to be let go; for the otherness.

Well. A Pandora's box-full of stagnant pre-occupations to be cleared away; for the clear in-sight hear-say testimony in act to 'rouse up and fix.' Williams's sight of Curie working at the muddle of pitchblende / one's apprehension of the secret energies of the speech. To clear away one's own secrets [the miasma] toward the work at the source – all the contained human energies of the language.

The mythic content has been released to use – Freud, Joyce, Pound, [. . .] Jane Harrison, Cassirer – plenty of ready work done. Stevens' demonstrations of myth construction. Then you prodded well at my 'wisdom' (re. *Artists View*) toward the actual sense. (In Harrison's *Theseus* the effort was to point back of the seem of the myth to the actual, the [. . .] – thing done. Back of the reference to; to the taking place. And an observation re: energy inherent in her study – that the energy *is* in the thing done; appears as derived there from in the re-currences (the ritual reenactments), further derived (lessened) in the references there – to – the mythic constructions. But is embodied in the language – (Diff. between the act as contained in its words, as evoked by its

(energy)
words (a memory of that energy, seeming changed), as exploited in history (a reference to that energy).

Thus: I ex-Pound. And you will allow my delight in calling up your presence / company (tenuous only when I reflect upon the alternative of your actual company. And talking to, at, (tenuous against a vividly – with) you to release currents of my thought. It hardly stirs against, to break up – as I would – very old channels. I wld [. . .] at the least breath of its construct. To have a sight of Jerusalem.

As for instance – a flash-sight in / beyond E.P.'s old rut of *Social Credit* that the language is a social fund, an air, water, earth or fire, an elemental wealth in which we, any, all have a social credit: unbounded. To claim inspiration (in-breathing), currents, roots and light/ heat.

What a mud, – a pitchblende – those recalcitrant pamphlets are, a crisis where we are forced to all the demand (the unmoving backlog) wall of his mind we drive in spite of against. But then toward? To? And everything not there springs up to mind. To 'tell you what any knowing man of your city might, a letter carrier, say, or that doctor' – but 'if they dared afford to take the risk.'

Our joy is that impending – here – we called for it, it calls for us, that 'dared afford' grows, increases, changes over is – a necessity. No other out but to 'take the risk.'

And E.P. (they called him Cracker-box filosofer) driven to the risk, unprepared. But it is not an occasion for accomplishment, but a necessity that drives him, I, the letter carrier to write the pamphlet. To do it 'wrong,' to force the damn(nation) that the waters be released.

The task is there – beyond giving *testimony* that I recognized, at last, what you are about (given in the letter you forwarded to *Origin*) – to write out what these two books of yours point toward. And I mean to rouse up my mind and fix my attention. Done, you tell and I'll tell Creeley this is not in your services (not an affair of the sheer camaraderie) but obviously (no one ain't taken no intrust) a necessity. A what are we doing here. Can't distinguish twixt a critical task and an 'age-of-criticism cud-chewing cow-licking exercise, an old habit' – it's a sad day

a coming. If it is we [are] a literary movement with our fortunes
to win I gladly default. My ever omnipotent laziness is healthy
instinctual recourse there. But if it is there might be, even if only
in – as if accident – an ascendance, a spark from that flinty task
to arouse us, get a move on, it's to be done.

I have in mind mimeographing said summing up of your
work – say circa 200 copies to be mailed out to a critical 'elite'
of readers – I mean those letter carriers and doktors where we
have come to recognize their readiness.

'In the third place the third capital is aroused' – Stein

yrs for a call to arms

R.D.[74]

***

Robert Duncan followed Creeley to Black Mountain in 1956,
very near the end of the experiment. He too had an earlier experience of the college, spending a very brief moment as a student
in 1938. He later recalled,

> I had not been there since sometime in 1938 when,
> having written from Berkeley I received an acceptance
> as a student and, as I remember, a part scholarship,
> and, precariously, set out, arriving there late one night,
> only to be turned away after the following day, firmly,
> with the notification by the instructor who had wel-
> comed me that I was found to be emotionally unfit.
> Was it after the heated argument I got into the morn-
> ing of that day concerning the Spanish Civil War? In

my anarchist convictions, the Madrid government seemed to me much the enemy as Franco was.[75]

When Duncan returned in 1956, Olson was rector of the college. The two poets had been engaged in their own intense correspondence, and Duncan viewed Olson as a major influence. He vowed to follow Olson into new activities of poetry, signalled by Olson's projective verse.

In *The H.D. Book* – a legendary collection of writings started in 1959, yet only properly published in book form in 2011– Duncan conjures transformative experiences under the stars, naming constellations, to summon the impact of Olson and Black Mountain:

> The figure of the giant hunter in the sky brings with it, as often, the creative genius of Charles Olson for me. Since the appearance of *Origin* I a decade ago, my vision of what the poem is to do has been transformed, reorganized around a constellation of new poets – Olson, Denise Levertov, Robert Creeley – in which Olson's work takes the lead for me. This man, himself a 'giant' – six foot seven or so – has been an outrider, my own Orion.
>
> It was the same time of year, with Orion overhead, in 1955, when Olson read aloud to Jess and me the beginnings of a new sequence of poems, *O'Ryan*. The scene in the bare room at Black Mountain with its cold and the blazing winter sky at the window springs up as I write. The fugitive hero of that sequence was drawn from Robert Creeley [. . .].[76]

At Black Mountain, Duncan taught poetry and theatre. As part of Olson's plan to create a 'college on wheels' after the closure of the North Carolina campus, Duncan undertook establishing a Black Mountain theatre company in San Francisco. Truly, it was in Northern California that Duncan began to develop his unique, prophetic voice as a poet in the 1940s. He was an integral part of the 'Berkeley Renaissance' and the Bay Area arts scene, along with his partner, Jess. But his activities at Black Mountain brought him into contact with ideas and pedagogical practices he could not have picked up anywhere else.

It was also at Black Mountain that Duncan completed many of the poems later collected in his book, *The Opening of the Field* (1960). With the additional influence of Jess's collage works, Duncan pushed Olson's ideas of *composition by field* even further, envisioning the poem as a 'grand collage' in which any and all activities of the poet – aesthetic, intellectual, visual, emotional, sexual, pedagogical, etc. – would interact.

In what is probably Duncan's most widely read poem from *The Opening of the Field*, he offers a stirring vision of this new space (place) open for the poet and poetry:

'Often I am permitted to Return to a Meadow'

as if it were a scene made-up by the mind,
that is not mine, but is a made place,

that is mine, it is so near to the heart,
an eternal pasture folded in all thought
so that there is a hall therein

that is a made place, created by light
wherefrom the shadows that are forms fall.

This is a box with nothing inside but the inside inside.

Dan's address:
213 Pearl St.
NY, NY

General Delivery
Alameda, NM
November 16, 1958

Dear Ed [Dorn],

I was reading that long poem of yours re yr mother, I have had for years etc: it's very like my mother in law, – and god willing will one day appear. I.e., things have been impossible regarding $$$, and as yet there is not much hope of getting out another issue. But Jonathan wrote last week about trying to start another magazine, twice a year – it seems ER irritates him & that is good – 128 pp or abt that, and who knows: perhaps. Have you sent that poem around elsewhere? It ought to damn well get printed before we are all old and dead and bits & pieces etc. Ok.

What are you doing? It's an impossible scene of bits & pieces already, with 3 courses (horses, forces, bourses, mabel etc) at Night:

> At night
> I see the light
> I am afright–
> ted, etc.

English 5280b – the being b, depends you see, : how are you Eddie boy, howr yer making It. Etc. Hearty handshake, harf harf: bull yer. Viz, go son: make the Aceodemic: ach, viz aches Only When I Sit Down, etcl: ecetlee, viz et-settle her, Un-settled. Settee – it all comes back to yr point o' vision: I see/ a settee.

In my mind's eye, of course. I (doctor) am continually beset by image I am tired and should (sewed, sued) set (beset, settled, suttee . . .) Down (dad) but that's what I am tired from (fro, fru * go in & out the rainbow, go in & out the rainbarrel). And pieces navel dripping from the sea. The blood you wore the last we 'twere engaged . . .

Anyhow we are making it, and how we are 'making it': Douglas Woolf told me he had bilt himself a cardboard house within his house: viz illustrative of Yr common function of Yr common metaphor, etc. Go dumborn dad, tell them's that wastes yr time & me, etc.

Ite, liber que no hablar: dige quibus, etc.

I wanted 'Ed' to write. God & all the saints preserve me. I mean, I want to write you – goddamnit. It is snowing, the desert, the place here, like they say, is awash with same – Yr dust & damned small indeed particles of frozen water. (9 odd chickens huddled out in the Gt/ Beyond: Our Responsibility). I am writing ok, ok. I never have excuse for silence, it droppeth as the gentle rain from heaven/ upon Yr leaking roof.

MY LOVE

It falleth like a stick.
   It lieth like air.
It is wonderment and bewilderment,
   to test true.

It is no thing, but of two,
   equal: as the mind turns to it,
it doubleth,
   as one alone.

Where it is, there is
     everywhere, separate,
yet few – as dew
     to night is.

We survive enuf. Life goes on, also enuf. Bit by bit I begin to construct something of it all, not a goddamn self-improvement or dam self denial, etc. Write, please. It's a favor I be asking. Ok.

     All love to you all,

          Bob

          [Creeley][77]

A BIBLIOGRAPHY ON AMERICA FOR ED DORN

     Assumptions: (1) that politics & economics (that is, agriculture,
                     fisheries, capital and labor) are like love (can
                     only be individually experienced and therefore, as
                     they have been presented (again, like love) are not
                     much use, that is, any study of the books about

              (2) that sociology, without exception, is a lot of
                     shit - produced by people who are the most dead
                     of all, history as politics or economics each
                     being at least events and laws, not this dread-
                     full beast, some average and/ statistic

Working premises:

   I   That millenia /
                    are not the same as either time as history
& II persons   /   or as the individual as single

                                In other words,

that plural & quality (taste) - King Numbers & King Shit - obscure

how it is.

      And that one must henceforth apply to quantity as a principle

(totally displacing hierarchies of taste or quality, as though there were

any other "like" than an attention which has completely saturated or circum-

vented the object);

         and to process as the most interesting fact of fact (the over-

whelming one, how it works, not what, in that what is always different if

the thing or person or event under review is a live one, and is different

because adverbally it is changing) -

                one must henceforth apply to quantity

as a principle and to process as the most interesting fact all attention

Results, as of historical study:

                     (a) it is not how much one knows but
in what field of context it is retained, and used (millenia, & quantity)

                     (b) how, as yrself as individual, you
are acquiring & using same in acts of form - what use you are making of
acquired information (person, & process)

THE ABOVE, IN OUTLINE FORM, IS A TABLE OF CONTENTS. The PREFACE is to follow.

From Olson's 'Bibliography on America for Ed Dorn'

Federal Bureau – Black Mountain Rag

This investigation

was predicated upon

was absent from

the institution indicates

that the survey submitted

in behalf of veterans indicated

periods of enrollment

perfect attendance

the summary report advised

respect to possible fraud

on the basis of information

arrange for a conference

requested that an Agent

be present make

all necessary records available

but keeps no record

This office will open individual cases

resulted in the school's approval

contemplates prosecution

and requests additional investigation

There is no misunderstanding

the procedure of these matters

irregularities indicated

discussion with the United States Attorney

doubt as to the accuracy

and truthfulness of

information described above

BLACK MOUNTAIN COLLEGE

NORTH CAROLINA certificates indicated

not yet interviewed

presently outside this Division

Do not write in spaces below Bureau

This investigation was predicated upon receipt

Approved

Copies made

Special Agent in Charge

USA

was absent from the institution

AT ASHEVILLE

Western District

Dates of Attendance

Total Amount Subsistence

No. Days Per Week

While there may seem some laxity

in the keeping of records

Finally, I am unawares

I have read this statement

it is true

_____ further advised

what pertains to preparing booklets

of poetry composed by himself

free of charge this type of poetry

not engaged in the commercial sense

that he has never received any

compensation, with the exception

I make the above voluntary statement

I am of age and I can read and write

the English language

these hours totaled irregularly

I have read the above statement

It is true

the facts of this case were discussed

necessary to show facts indefinite

indicating on a regular basis

He felt the facts developed

he believed that no further investigation

was necessary that he would decline

I have read the above statement

it is true

I met the German artist Astrid Kaemmerling for the first time at Black Mountain. She was then living in Ohio, and we had both come to North Carolina to speak at a conference in Asheville. I sensed immediate affinity.

Astrid spoke of Black Mountain with sure intelligence, and with the insight of an artist. Our meeting at Black Mountain initiated a correspondence that has been vital to me over the last several years – stretching far across the world from Ireland to where she now lives in San Francisco.

The first drawings Astrid enclosed in a letter set my poems to a visual field. I recognized at once the Black Mountain aura, but with a subtle touch that made the college new. In her collages, paintings, and drawings, Astrid captures – with uncanny accuracy – the physical and emotional circumstances of my writing.

She has rooted them all in Black Mountain. Our own correspondence is rooted there, at an indefinable centre between transatlantic poles.

When I moved to Berlin, a greeting reached me from Astrid in California. There are no stretches of SPACE now such as there were for Olson, Albers, Rice, Creeley, and Duncan. Or for Pound, Williams, Dickinson, and Melville, for that matter.

These were the points of contact, our areas of departure.

Astrid and I next came together to collaborate at the Black Mountain College {Re}Happening. The event was organized by BMCM+AC in Asheville, inviting artists to the Lake Eden campus to recreate, in spirit, the circumstances of John Cage's original happening in the dining hall.

Astrid and I collaborated with the artists Danielle Wyckoff from Michigan and Mark Bloch from New York City. Mark had known Ray Johnson and John Cage. We combined performance, text, painting, and music to create an interactive space on the old grounds of the college. From our ends of the earth, we met at Black Mountain – came together around Lake Eden, and returned changed for the depth of experience we found there.

There is no use in explaining. To be there. To create it again.

Work exhibited at {Re}Happening (Jonathan C. Creasy)

As artists we instinctively search for sympathetic company: 'a few other golden ears,' as Allen Ginsberg said. This drive started early in me, and it continues. My mother taught the Transcendentalists, another imperfect company of frustrated philosophers, writers, Americans. That drive of theirs led to an experiment we can look at as precursor to Black Mountain.

Brook Farm (1841–1847) – an initial experiment – was fictionalized in Nathaniel Hawthorne's *The Blithedale Romance*:

> Therefore, if we built splendid castles (phalansteries, perhaps, they might be more fitly called,) and pictured beautiful scenes, among the fervid coals of the hearth around which we were clustering – and if all went to rack with the crumbling embers, and have never since arisen out of the ashes – let us take to ourselves no shame. In my own behalf, I rejoice that I could once think better of the world's improvability than it deserved. It is a mistake into which men seldom fall twice, in a lifetime; or, if so, the rarer and higher is the nature that can thus magnanimously persist in error.[78]

Our efforts are errors of order. Our company persists despite misfortune and failure. I set out searching, not knowing what was there, and found in Black Mountain the company I keep.

***

In the manner of Creeley's letters to Pound and Williams, one day I ventured a correspondence with Susan Howe. She had taught in the University at Buffalo poetics program after Olson and alongside Creeley, so I went to Howe in order to access the poet as teacher. The happy surprise of her response, and afterward her continued interest and friendship, matches what

I imagine Creeley's pleasure must have been in corresponding with Williams.

Several times now I have visited Susan at her home in Connecticut. On one particularly pleasurable occasion, we shared dinner with Richard Deming, Nancy Kuhl, and Elizabeth Willis. Such company makes one feel the confidence of elective affinity. I go on searching through stacks and archives, through history and poetry, and I know that in these trespasses I rejoice in the world's imaginative possibilities. Black Mountain was a series of ambitious mistakes. Into these mistakes I gladly fall again and again.

Haunting voices of the past break through into the present. Borders dissolve. Ireland is vivid in Susan's poetic imagination; it is the ancestral homeland. In a 2012 *Paris Review* interview, she claims, 'I've always felt a tremendous pull between Ireland and America, because of my parents – my mother being Irish, and my father being a New Englander from Boston. I felt torn between them – in the sense of allegiance to the word.' When I met Susan, she reminded me of my divided world – the split between home and away, and the difficulty in seeing which one is which.

She knows Olson's pronouncement, 'poets are the only pedagogues.' She and Creeley practiced as much together.

Susan is my spiritual link to Black Mountain, as close as I will come to personal poetic contact. Her perception of shades in the living world, here on earth, where we carve out quarries and read poems for sound's echoing sense, has given back to me a kind of mother: 'Oh for that night when the absent parent will restore order by covering the child with a seamless shroud so that wrath is never the last thread in the fold.'[79]

And so on into Silence.

From Asheville's Smoky Mountains to New England, from Berlin to Dublin, I have searched for Black Mountain in the wilds of material archives and over the range of artistic interactions.

Here are the shadows cast by Black Mountain across the century.

This is the poetic vision of my ordinary life, before and after.

Here are the phalansteries we build out of poems.

Here is a singular portrait of history.

A song, as a bird's – some ancient, elliptical music.

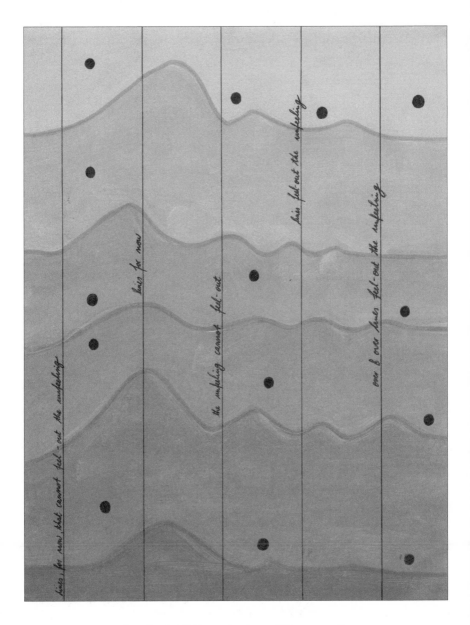

Songbirds of Cergy, by Astrid Kaemmerling
(in correspondence with the author)

Elegy

We had faith in the turns of your foundation.
What we've buried now, to a world magnificent
in space, in perjury of time, and in will – sheer will.

Take easy the tide, cold still with summer.
A vengeance of these wilds, walking over,
breathless, heedless, south of all borders.

A service to the godhead; he remarked
on your *Over Soul* – these were parodies
of your once so righteous conditions.

Take a nickel or a dime for my vocation.
I have learned it; it's had its use for me.
Guided as we were by indecision – taught

Improvisation. We had faith in the turns of
your foundation. What we've buried now,
to a world magnificent in song, we are ended.

Jonathan C. Creasy
Black Mountain – Berlin – New York – Dublin
2016

Acknowledgements

So many people have been important to the process of this book. My father, Dr. William Creasy, was the first intellectual example I had, and I certainly would not have made my way to this writing without him. His support and his discipline made my life, as it is, possible. And my brother, Dr. Adam Creasy, has been the solid foundation of our family and, I suppose, always will be.

Dr. Philip Coleman, my friend and mentor at Trinity College Dublin, saw promise in my study of Black Mountain College. He supervised my PhD research and did so with even-handed kindness and encouragement. He is a fine reader, critic, and poetic companion. Others at Trinity have lent their support over the years: Maria Johnston, Gerald Dawe, Deirdre Madden, Stephen Matterson, Orla McCarthy, Diane Sadler, Alex Runchman, Gillian Groszewski, Jane Alden, Helen Shenton, and Darryl Jones. Eve Cobain kept me engaged with poems, wine, and food, making the perfect partner in the PhD push.

Parts of *The Black Mountain Letters* appeared in various publications over the years, and I am grateful to all those editors who took interest: sections of 'Asheville [Archive]' were published in *Dublin Review of Books*. The Black Mountain College Project at Freie Universität Berlin published various pieces during the period of my DAAD scholarship. I am very grateful to Annette Lehmann for her guidance in Berlin, and to Ulrich Schwarz for setting a remarkable example and being such a friend in Germany. 'Dakota Dream [unsung]' appeared in *Berryman's Fate*, an anthology edited by Philip Coleman and published by Arlen House.

I have had help from some extraordinary people in archives around the world: Heather South at the Western Regional Branch of the State Archives in Asheville, North Carolina; Melissa Watterworth Batt at the University of Connecticut's Dodd Research Center; Nina Schönig and Wencke Clausnitzer at the *Bauhaus-Archiv* in Berlin; and Nancy Kuhl at the Beinecke Rare Books Library.

I have made my debt to certain writers and artists abundantly clear, but Susan Howe, Vincent Katz, Astrid Kaemmerling, Nerys Williams, Peter Erskine, Jeff Hamilton, Matt Wilson, Clayton Cameron, Aaron Smith, Ernest Hilbert, Kimberly Campanello, Benjamin Dwyer, Rossi McAuley, Richard Deming, Myles Dungan, Giles Clark, and Martin Nevin need to be thanked again. Correspondence and friendship with them have been endlessly rewarding and have shaped my artistic life.

To all those in the Black Mountain community. First of all, Mary Emma Harris. The rest of us would know very little without her work, and her kindness and support have been crucial to this book. Alice Sebrell and Erin Dickey at the Black Mountain College Museum + Arts Center in Asheville are so important to the continuing life of BMC. Other Asheville friends and colleagues: Jeff Davis, Brian Butler, Julie Thomson, Jay Miller, Alli Marshal at Mountain Xpress, and all the wonderful places to eat, drink, and sing in Asheville.

Pierre, Dominique, Joyce, Jessica, and Carol in Paris have my love and appreciation. They are a remarkable bunch, and I am privileged to count them among my family.

My deepest gratitude goes to Eimear Fallon, my love and life – she has stuck with me through this entire period. I owe her just about more than I can say. And to our Jack, a grounding presence.

With love and admiration for you all.

About the Author

Jonathan C. Creasy was born and raised in Los Angeles, California, where his father taught in the English Department at UCLA and his mother was the Department Chair in English at Brentwood School. As a child, Creasy travelled the world, primarily in the Middle East. He was baptized in the Jordan River and later became a Junior National Diving champion.

Creasy studied music with jazz legends Peter Erskine and Jeff Hamilton. After graduating high school, he went on to study music under Charlie Haden at California Institute of the Arts (CalArts) and performed and recorded music throughout California and the United States.

In 2007, he moved to Ireland to study literature at Trinity College Dublin, graduating with First Class Honours. At Trinity, he was Poetry Editor of *Icarus* magazine. In 2011–2012, he taught writing in the Undergraduate Writing Center at the University of Texas at Austin, and in 2012 returned to Ireland to pursue PhD research in the School of English at Trinity College. The same year, he founded New Dublin Press, for which he serves as Editor-in-Chief and Publisher. He continues to perform and record as a musician, while teaching literature and writing in several institutions in Ireland.

In 2015, Creasy was awarded a DAAD Scholarship by the German government to pursue research in Berlin at the Bauhaus Archive. While in Germany, he worked with Annette Jael Lehmann at Freie Universität Berlin and architect and designer Ulrich Schwarz, Dean of Visual Communications at Universität der Künste Berlin. Creasy has also worked in radio, appearing regularly on RTÉ Radio 1, Ireland's national broadcaster. In 2016, he was awarded the Lannan Writing Residency by the Lannan Foundation. He divides his time between his home in Dublin and various locations in the United States and Europe.

Bibliography

Albers, Josef. *Interaction of Color: 50th Anniversary Edition*. Yale University Press, 2013.

——— and Nicholas Fox Weber. *Poems and Drawings*. Yale University Press, 2006.

Albright, Alex, ed. *North Carolina Literary Review: The Black Mountain College Issue*. Volume 11. Number 2. East Carolina University, 1995.

Allen, Donald, ed. *The New American Poetry 1945-1960*. University of California Press, 2012.

Archer, Hazel Larsen. *Black Mountain College Photographer*. Asheville: Black Mountain College Museum + Arts Center, 2006.

Benfey, Christopher. *Red Brick, Black Mountain, White Clay*. Penguin Books, 2013.

Butler, Brian. ed. *Dan Rice at Black Mountain College: Painter Among Poets*. Asheville: Black Mountain College Museum + Arts Center, 2014.

Butterick, George F. *A Guide to the Maximus Poems of Charles Olson*. Berkeley: University of California Press, 1978.

———, ed. *OLSON: The Journal of the Charles Olson Archive*. University of Connecticut, 1974.

Cage, John. *Silence: Lecture and Writings, 50th Anniversary Edition*. Wesleyan, 2011.

———. *A Year From Monday: New Lectures and Writings*. Wesleyan, 1967.

———. *Composition in Retrospect*. Cambridge: Exact Change, 1993.

———. *Diary: How to Improve the World (You Will Only Make Matters Worse)*. Siglio, 2015.

———. *The Selected Letters of John Cage*. ed. Laura Kuhn. Wesleyan, 2016.

———. *M: Writings '67-'72*. Wesleyan, 1973.

Cappellazzo, Amy and Elizabeth Licata, eds. *In Company: Robert*

Creeley's Collaborations. University of North Carolina Press, 1999.

Clark, Tom. *Robert Creeley and the Genius of the American Common Place*. New Directions, 1993.

———. *Charles Olson: Allegory of a Poet's Life*. W.W. Norton, 1991.

———. *Edward Dorn: A World of Difference*. North Atlantic Books, 2002.

Creeley, Robert and Charles Olson. *Collected Correspondence (Ten Volumes)*. Ed. George F. Butterick. Black Sparrow Press, 1980.

Creeley, Robert. *Selected Poems*. University of California Press, 1996.

———. *The Selected Letters of Robert Creeley*. University of California Press, 2014.

———. *Collected Poems 1945-1975*. University of California Press, 2006.

———. *Collected Poems 1975-2005*. University of California Press, 2008.

———. *Collected Prose*. Dalkey Archive Press, 2001.

———. *Collected Essays*. University of California Press, 1989.

———. *Was That a Real Poem & other essays*. Bolinas: Four Seasons, 1979.

Dahlberg, Edward. *Can These Bones Live*. New York: New Directions, 1960.

Dawson, Fielding. *The Black Mountain Book*. North Carolina Wesleyan, 1991.

Dewey, John. *On Education: Selected Writings*. University of Chicago Press, 1974.

Diaz, Eva. *The Experimenters: Chance and Design at Black Mountain College*. University of Chicago Press, 2014.

Dorn, Edward. *Collected Poems*. Carcanet, 2012.

———. *Gunslinger*. London: Duke University Press, 1989.

Droste, Magdalena. *bauhaus: bauhaus archive*. Taschen, 2013.

Duberman, Martin. *Black Mountain College: An Exploration in*

Community. North Western University Press, 2009. (reprint)

Duncan, Robert. *Selected Poems*. New Directions, 1997.

———. *A Poet's Mind: Collected Interviews 1960-1985*. North Atlantic Books, 2012.

———. *Ground Work: Before the War / In the Dark*. New York: New Directions, 2006.

———. *The Opening of the Field*. New Directions, 1973.

———. *Roots and Branches*. New Directions, 1969.

———. *The HD Book*. University of California Press, 2011.

Foster, Edward Halsey. *Understanding the Black Mountain Poets*. University of South Carolina, 1994.

Harris, Mary Emma. *The Arts at Black Mountain College*. The MIT Press, 2002.

———. *Remembering Black Mountain College*. Asheville: Black Mountain College Museum + Arts Center, 1995.

Hawthorne, Nathaniel. *The Blithedale Romance*. The Modern Library Classics, 2001.

Herd, David, ed. *Contemporary Olson*. Manchester University Press, 2015.

Horowitz, Frederick and Brenda Danilowitz, eds. *Josef Albers: To Open Eyes*. Phaidon Press, 2009.

Howe, Susan. *The Birth-Mark: Unsettling the Wilderness in American Literary History*. New York: New Directions, 2015.

———. *Spontaneous Particulars: The Telepathy of Archives*. New York: New Directions, 2014.

———. *The Quarry*. New York: New Directions, 2015.

Katz, Vincent, ed. *Black Mountain College: Experiment in Art*. The MIT Press, 2013.

Laughlin, James. *Pound as Wuz: Essays and Lectures on Ezra*. Graywolf Press, 1987.

Lawrence, D. H. *Studies in Classic American Literature. Viking Compass Books*, 1951.

Le Corbusier. *Towards a Modern Architecture*. Dover Publications, 1985.

Levertov, Denise. *Selected Poems*. New Directions, 2003.

Levertov, Denise & Robert Duncan. *The Letters of Denise Levertov and Robert Duncan*. Stanford University Press, 2003.

Lupton, Ellen and J. Abbott Miller, eds. *The ABCs of the Bauhaus and Design Theory*. London: Thames & Hudson, 2000.

Maud, Ralph. *Charles Olson at the Harbor*. Talonbooks, 2008.

Molesworth, Helen. *Leap Before You Look: Black Mountain College 1933-1957*. Yale University Press, 2015.

Moody, A. David. *Ezra Pound: Poet*. (Vols. I-III) Oxford University Press, 2007 / 2014 / 2015.

Morley, Hilda. *The Turning*. Moyer Bell, 2003.

Oppenheimer, Joel. *Name & Local Habitations*. Jargon Society, 1988.

Olson, Charles. *Selected Writings of Charles Olson*. Ed. Robert Creeley. New Directions, 1997.

———. *The Archaeologist of Morning*. Grossman, 1973.

———. *Collected Prose*. University of California Press, 1997.

———. *Charles Olson & Ezra Pound: Encounters at St. Elizabeths*. Paragon House, 1991.

———. *Call Me Ishmael*. London: Johns Hopkins University Press, 1997.

———. *Muthologos: Lectures and Interviews*. Ed. Ralph Maud Talonbooks, 2010.

———. *The Special View of History*. Oyez, 1970.

Paul, Sherman. *Olson's Push: Origin, Black Mountain and Recent American Poetry*. Louisiana State University Press, 1978.

Pound, Ezra. *The ABC of Reading*. New York: New Directions, 1934.

———. *The Cantos of Ezra Pound*. New York: New Directions, 1996.

———. *Guide to Kulchur*. New York: New Directions, 1970.

———. *Literary Essays*. London: Faber & Faber, 1961.

Rice, John Andrew. *I Came Out of the Eighteenth Century*. University of South Carolina, 2014.

Richards, M. C. *The Crossing Point: Selected Talks and Writings*. Wesleyan, 1973.

————. *Centering in Pottery, Poetry, and the Person.* Wesleyan, 1989.

Rumaker, Michael. *Black Mountain Days.* Spuyten Duyvil, 2012.

Sargent, Porter. *Between Two Wars: The Failure of Education 1920–1940.* Porter Sargent Publishing, 1945.

Weber, Nicholas Fox. *The Bauhaus Group: Six Masters of Modernism.* Yale University Press, 2011.

Whitehead, Alfred North. *The Aims of Education.* London: Williams & Norgate, 1951.

————. *Process and Reality.* Free Press (2nd Edition), 1979.

Wieners, John. *Supplication: Selected Poems.* Enitharmon Press, 2015.

Williams, Jonathan. *An Ear in Bartram's Tree: Selected Poems 1957-1967.* New Directions, 1969.

Williams, William Carlos. *The Autobiography of William Carlos Williams.* New York: New Directions, 1951.

————. *The Collected Poems: 1939–1962.* New York: New Directions, 1991.

————. *In the American Grain.* New York: New Directions, 2009.

————. *Paterson (Revised Edition).* New York: New Directions, 1995.

————. *The Selected Letters of W.C.W.* New York: New Directions, 1957.

————. *Spring and All (Facsimile Edition).* New York: New Directions, 2011.

Yao, Steven G. and Michael Coyle, eds. *Ezra Pound and Education.* National Poetry Foundation, 2012.

Notes

(Endnotes)

[1] Olson, Charles and Robert Creeley. *The Complete Correspondence.* Black Sparrow Press, 1985. Reprinted with permission from Godine Publishing.

[2] *Bulletin of the American Association of University Professors*, Vol. XIX, No. 7 (November, 1933) 426

[3] Duberman, Martin. *Black Mountain: An Exploration in Community.* New York: Dutton & Co. 1972. 22 (hereafter: Duberman).

[4] Harris, Mary Emma. *The Arts at Black Mountain College.* MIT Press, 2002. 4 (hereafter: Harris).

[5] Harris 5

[6] Dewey, John. *On Education: Selected Writings.* University of Chicago Press, 1974. 11

[7] Dewey, John. 'American Art and Education.' *On Education: Selected Writings.* 291 / 294

[8] Originally published in *Charles Olson & Robert Creeley: The Complete Correspondence.* Black Sparrow Press. Reprinted with permission from Godine Publishing.

[9] From materials found in the Western Regional Branch of the North Carolina State Archives. With thanks to archivist Heather South and published by permission of the State Archives.

[10] FBI file on Black Mountain College. As reported in the Carolina Public Press, August 5, 2015, "The FBI scrutinized Black Mountain College". Investigative reporter Jon Elliston filed a Freedom of Information request to obtain the documents. All of the memoranda can be found here: http://www .documentcloud.org/documents/2191031-bmcfbifile.html

[11] Originally published in *Charles Olson & Robert Creeley: The Complete Correspondence.* Black Sparrow Press. Reprinted with permission from Godine Publishing.

[12] Feininger, Lyonel (1871-1956) © ARS, NY. Cathedral (Kathedrale) for Program of the State Bauhaus in Weimar (Programm des Staatlichen Bauhauses in Weimar). 1919. Woodcut, composition: 12 x 7 1/2" Publisher: Staatliches Bauhaus, Weimar. Printer: the artist. Edition: state I: approx. 6-15 proofs before the edition of

an unknown number for the "Program of the State Bauhaus in Weimar". Gift of Aldrich Rockefeller. The Museum of Modern Art. Digital Image © The Museum of Modern Art

[13] Josef Albers quoted in Weber, Nicholas Fox. *The Bauhaus Group: Six Masters of Modernism*. Yale University Press, 2011. 337

[14] Droste, Magdalena. *Bauhaus: Bauhaus Archiv: 1919-1933*. TASCHEN, 2013. 25

[15] © Yamawaki Iwao & Michiko Archives, reprinted with permission.

[16] This and the following quotations come from the unpublished correspondence between Ted Dreier and Walter Gropius, found in the *Bauhaus-Archiv* and printed here with their permission.

[17] Ted Dreier's 'Summary Report – Black Mountain College: the First 15 1/2 Years,' found in the Gropius Papers, *Bauhaus-Archiv*.

[18] Albers quoted in Harris 53

[19] Katz, Vincent. *Black Mountain College: An Experiment in Art*. MIT Press, 2013

[20] Horowitz, Frederick A. and Brenda Danilowitz. *Josef Albers: To Open Eyes*. Phaedon Press, 2009. Introduction.

[21] Horowitz 10

[22] Horowitz 12

[23] Dewey 7

[24] Harris 16

[25] Horowitz 14

[26] Henry Miller quoted in Harris 47

[27] Robert Duncan quoted in Jarnot, Lisa. *Robert Duncan, The Ambassador from Venus*. University of California Press, 2012. 154

[28] Charles Olson Letter to Ping Ferry. *OLSON: The Journal of the Charles Olson Archive*. University of Connecticut. Number 2: Fall 1974. 8

[29] Duberman, Martin. *Black Mountain College: An Exploration in Community*. Dutton, 1972. 53-54 (hereafter: Duberman.)

[30] Duberman 15

[31] Duberman 16

[32] Olson to Ping Ferry, *Ibid*.

[33] © 2015 The Josef and Anni Albers Foundation (With thanks to Nicholas Fox Weber and Brenda Danilowitz.)

[34] © Estate of Xanti Schawinsky. Reproduced with permission from Daniel Schawinsky

[35] Williams, William Carlos. 'Author's Introductions to *The Wedge* (1944).' *Selected Essays*. New Directions, 1969. 255

[36] Laughlin, James. *Pound as Wuz*. Peter Owen Publishers, 1989. 34

[37] *Pound and Education*. ed. Yao, Steven and Coyle, Michael. National Poetry Foundation, 2012. intro xiv

[38] *Pound as Wuz* 4

[39] Moody, A. David. *Ezra Pound: Poet*. Oxford University Press, 2009. 33

[40] Golding, Alan. 'From Pound to Olson: The Avant-Garde Poet as Pedagogue.' *Pound and Education*, 187

[41] Pound, Ezra. 'Teacher's Mission' *Literary Essays*. New Directions, 1968. 59

[42] 'Teacher's Mission' 62

[43] Reprinted in Tom Clark's *Robert Creeley and the Genius of the American Common Place*. New Directions, 1993. 137

[44] Sargent, Porter. *Between Two Wars: The Failure of Education 1920-1940*. Porter Sargent Publishing, 1945. 18 / 23

[45] Sargent 153

[46] Moody 33

[47] Sargent 487

[48] Sargent 56

[49] Sargent 56

[50] Creeley, Robert. *Was That a Real Poem and Other Essays*. Ed. Donald Allen. Bolinas: Four Seasons Foundation, 1964. 74

[51] Olson, Charles. (ed. Catherine Seelye) *Charles Olson and Ezra Pound: An Encounter at St. Elizabeths*. Paragon House, 1991. 15

[52] *An Encounter at St. Elizabeths*. 16

[53] Clark, Tom. *Charles Olson: The Allegory of a Poet's Life*. North Atlantic Books, 2000.

[54] Maximus Letter 27 withheld

[55] Olson, Charles. *Call Me Ishmael*.

[56] Howe, Susan. 'Where Should the Commander Be?' *The Quarry*, 2015.

[57] Creeley, Robert. 'The Black Mountain Review.' *Collected Essays*. Berkeley: University of California Press, 1989. 507

[58] Creeley, Robert. 'Olson & Others: Some Orts for the Sports.' *The New American Poetry 1945-1960*. ed. Donald Allen. Berkeley: University of California Press, 1999. 409

[59] Creeley, Robert. 'Preface.' Tom Clark. *The Allegory of a Poet's Life.* North Atlantic Books, 2000.

[60] Olson Charles, 'On Black Mountain.' *Muthologos: Lectures and Interviews.* ed. Ralph Maud. Talonbooks, 2010.

[61] Olson, Charles. *Projective Verse.*

[62] Whitehead Aims of Education 1-2

[63] Ibid 2

[64] Ibid 9

[65] 'A Draft of a Plan for the College.' *OLSON: The Journal of the Charles Olson Archives.* University of Connecticut. Number 2, Fall 1974.

[66] 'Introduction.' *Contemporary Olson.* ed. David Herd. Manchester University Press, 2015.

[67] 'LETTER 6.' *The Maximus Poems.* ed. Charles F. Butterick. University of California Press, 1985. 32

[68] Butterick, George F. 'Editor's Introduction.' *Charles Olson and Robert Creeley: The Complete Correspondence.* Volume I. Black Sparrow Press, 1980.

[69] Duberman 386

[70] Creeley, Robert. 'Black Mountain Review.' *Was That a Real Poem & Other Essays.* Bolinas: Four Seasons Foundation. 1979. 16-28.

[71] Copies of *The Black Mountain Review* are held in the collections of the Thomas J. Dodd Research Center at the University of Connecticut. The author has made visits to the Dodd collections to look at BMR and related archives, particularly the Olson / Creeley correspondence and material related to Olson's work as final rector of the college.

[72] Exhibition: *Dan Rice at Black Mountain College: A Painter Among Poets.* Black Mountain College Museum + Arts Center. Asheville, N.C. Sept. 2014 – January 2015. Curator, Brian Butler. (See Butler's exhibition catalogue, with essays, of the same title)

[73] This is an expurgated, transcribed selection from the following recording: Creeley, Robert. 'Response to Martin Duberman's interview questions on Black Mountain, from the late 1960s.' Courtesy Jeff Davis. Recording from North Carolina Division of Archives and History. (Transcript a selection by the author.) For the full recording, visit Pennsound: http://writing.upenn.edu/pennsound/x/Creeley.php

[74] Letter from Robert Duncan to Charles Olson: June 17, 1954. © 2015 The Jess Collins Trust

[75] Duncan, Robert. *The HD Book*. ed. Boughn, Michael and Coleman, Victor. University of California Press, 2012.

[76] Ibid.

[77] Creeley, Robert. *The Selected Letters of Robert Creeley*. ed. Rod Smith, Peter Baker, and Kaplan Harris. Berkeley: University of California Press, 2014.

[78] Hawthorne, Nathaniel. *The Blithedale Romance*. Modern Library Classics, 2001.

[79] Howe, Susan. 'Vagrancy in the Park.' *The Quarry*. New York: New Direction, 201

MICHAL AJVAZ, *The Golden Age.*
The Other City.
PIERRE ALBERT-BIROT, *Grabinoulor.*
YUZ ALESHKOVSKY, *Kangaroo.*
FELIPE ALFAU, *Chromos.*
Locos.
ANTÓNIO LOBO ANTUNES, *Knowledge of Hell.*
The Splendor of Portugal.
JOHN ASHBERY & JAMES SCHUYLER, *A Nest of Ninnies.*
ROBERT ASHLEY, *Perfect Lives.*
GABRIELA AVIGUR-ROTEM, *Heatwave and Crazy Birds.*
DJUNA BARNES, *Ladies Almanack.*
Ryder.
DONALD BARTHELME, *The King.*
Paradise.
SVETISLAV BASARA, *Chinese Letter.*
RENÉ BELLETTO, *Dying.*
MAREK BIENCZYK, *Transparency.*
ANDREJ BLATNIK, *You Do Understand.*
Law of Desire.
IGNÁCIO DE LOYOLA BRANDÃO, *Anonymous Celebrity.*
Zero.
BONNIE BREMSER, *Troia: Mexican Memoirs.*
CHRISTINE BROOKE-ROSE, *Amalgamemnon.*
BRIGID BROPHY, *In Transit.*
The Prancing Novelist.
GERALD L. BRUNS, *Modern Poetry and the Idea of Language.*
GABRIELLE BURTON, *Heartbreak Hotel.*
MICHEL BUTOR, *Degrees.*
Mobile.
G. CABRERA INFANTE, *Infante's Inferno.*
Three Trapped Tigers.
JULIETA CAMPOS, *The Fear of Losing Eurydice.*
ANNE CARSON, *Eros the Bittersweet.*
ORLY CASTEL-BLOOM, *Dolly City.*
MARIE CHAIX, *The Laurels of Lake Constance.*

HUGO CHARTERIS, *The Tide Is Right.*
ERIC CHEVILLARD, *Demolishing Nisard.*
The Author and Me.
MARC CHOLODENKO, *Mordechai Schamz.*
EMILY HOLMES COLEMAN, *The Shutter of Snow.*
ERIC CHEVILLARD, *The Author and Me.*
ROBERT COOVER, *A Night at the Movies.*
STANLEY CRAWFORD, *Log of the S.S. The Mrs Unguentine.*
Some Instructions to My Wife.
RENÉ CREVEL, *Putting My Foot in It.*
PETER DIMOCK, *A Short Rhetoric for Leaving the Family.*
ARIEL DORFMAN, *Konfidenz.*
COLEMAN DOWELL, *Island People.*
Too Much Flesh and Jabez.
ARKADII DRAGOMOSHCHENKO, *Dust.*
RIKKI DUCORNET, *Phosphor in Dreamland.*
The Complete Butcher's Tales.
The Jade Cabinet.
The Fountains of Neptune.
JEAN ECHENOZ, *Chopin's Move.*
STANLEY ELKIN, *A Bad Man.*
Criers and Kibitzers, Kibitzers and Criers.
The Dick Gibson Show.
The Franchiser.
The Living End.
Mrs. Ted Bliss.
FRANÇOIS EMMANUEL, *Invitation to a Voyage.*
PAUL EMOND, *The Dance of a Sham.*
SALVADOR ESPRIU, *Ariadne in the Grotesque Labyrinth.*
LESLIE A. FIEDLER, *Love and Death in the American Novel.*
ANDY FITCH, *Pop Poetics.*
GUSTAVE FLAUBERT, *Bouvard and Pécuchet.*
MAX FRISCH, *I'm Not Stiller.*
Man in the Holocene.

CARLOS FUENTES, *Christopher Unborn.*
Distant Relations.
Terra Nostra.
Where the Air Is Clear.

TAKEHIKO FUKUNAGA, *Flowers of Grass.*

WILLIAM GADDIS, JR., *The Recognitions.*

JANICE GALLOWAY, *Foreign Parts.*
The Trick Is to Keep Breathing.

WILLIAM H. GASS, *Life Sentences.*
The Tunnel.
The World Within the Word.
Willie Masters' Lonesome Wife.

GÉRARD GAVARRY, *Hoppla! 1 2 3.*

ETIENNE GILSON, *The Arts of the Beautiful.*
Forms and Substances in the Arts.

C. S. GISCOMBE, *Giscome Road.*
Here.

WITOLD GOMBROWICZ, *A Kind of Testament.*

PAULO EMÍLIO SALES GOMES, *P's Three Women.*

GEORGI GOSPODINOV, *Natural Novel.*

JUAN GOYTISOLO, *Count Julian.*
Juan the Landless.
Makbara.
Marks of Identity.

JACK GREEN, *Fire the Bastards!*

JIŘÍ GRUŠA, *The Questionnaire.*

MELA HARTWIG, *Am I a Redundant Human Being?*

JOHN HAWKES, *The Passion Artist.*
Whistlejacket.

ELIZABETH HEIGHWAY, ED., *Contemporary Georgian Fiction.*

AIDAN HIGGINS, *Balcony of Europe.*
Blind Man's Bluff.
Bornholm Night-Ferry.
Langrishe, Go Down.
Scenes from a Receding Past.

KEIZO HINO, *Isle of Dreams.*

KAZUSHI HOSAKA, *Plainsong.*

MIKHEIL JAVAKHISHVILI, *Kvachi.*

GERT JONKE, *The Distant Sound.*
Homage to Czerny.
The System of Vienna.

JACQUES JOUET, *Mountain R.*
Savage.
Upstaged.

MIEKO KANAI, *The Word Book.*

YORAM KANIUK, *Life on Sandpaper.*

ZURAB KARUMIDZE, *Dagny.*

DANILO KIŠ, *The Attic.*
The Lute and the Scars.
Psalm 44.
A Tomb for Boris Davidovich.

ANITA KONKKA, *A Fool's Paradise.*

GEORGE KONRÁD, *The City Builder.*

TADEUSZ KONWICKI, *A Minor Apocalypse.*
The Polish Complex.

ANNA KORDZAIA-SAMADASHVILI, *Me, Margarita.*

MENIS KOUMANDAREAS, *Koula.*

ELAINE KRAF, *The Princess of 72nd Street.*

JIM KRUSOE, *Iceland.*

AYSE KULIN, *Farewell: A Mansion in Occupied Istanbul.*

EMILIO LASCANO TEGUI, *On Elegance While Sleeping.*

ERIC LAURRENT, *Do Not Touch.*

VIOLETTE LEDUC, *La Bâtarde.*

EDOUARD LEVÉ, *Autoportrait.*
Newspaper.
Suicide.
Works.

MARIO LEVI, *Istanbul Was a Fairy Tale.*

DEBORAH LEVY, *Billy and Girl.*

JOSÉ LEZAMA LIMA, *Paradiso.*

ROSA LIKSOM, *Dark Paradise.*

OSMAN LINS, *Avalovara.*
The Queen of the Prisons of Greece.

FLORIAN LIPUŠ, *The Errors of Young Tjaž.*

ALF MACLOCHLAINN, *Out of Focus.*
Past Habitual.
The Corpus in the Library.

RON LOEWINSOHN, *Magnetic Field(s).*

YURI LOTMAN, *Non-Memoirs.*

MINA LOY, *Stories and Essays of Mina Loy.*

MICHELINE AHARONIAN MARCOM,
A Brief History of Yes.
The Mirror in the Well.

DAVID MARKSON, *Reader's Block.*
Wittgenstein's Mistress.

CAROLE MASO, *AVA..*

HARRY MATHEWS, *Cigarettes.*
The Conversions.
The Human Country.
The Journalist.
My Life in CIA.
Singular Pleasures.
The Sinking of the Odradek.
Stadium.
Tlooth.

HISAKI MATSUURA, *Triangle.*

JOSEPH MCELROY, *Night Soul and Other Stories.*

ABDELWAHAB MEDDEB, *Talismano.*

AMANDA MICHALOPOULOU, *I'd Like.*

STEVEN MILLHAUSER, *The Barnum Museum.*
In the Penny Arcade.

CHRISTINE MONTALBETTI, *The Origin of Man.*
Western.

WARREN MOTTE, *Fables of the Novel: French Fiction since 1990.*
Fiction Now: The French Novel in the 21st Century.
Mirror Gazing.
Oulipo: A Primer of Potential Literature.

GERALD MURNANE, *Barley Patch.*
Inland.

YVES NAVARRE, *Our Share of Time.*
Sweet Tooth.

DOROTHY NELSON, *In Night's City.*
Tar and Feathers.

WILFRIDO D. NOLLEDO, *But for the Lovers.*

FLANN O'BRIEN, *At Swim-Two-Birds.*
The Best of Myles.
The Dalkey Archive.
The Hard Life.

The Poor Mouth.
The Third Policeman.

CLAUDE OLLIER, *The Mise-en-Scène.*
Wert and the Life Without End.

PATRIK OUŘEDNÍK, *Europeana.*
The Opportune Moment, 1855.

FERNANDO DEL PASO, *News from the Empire.*
Palinuro of Mexico.

ROBERT PINGET, *The Inquisitory.*
Mahu or The Material.
Trio.

MANUEL PUIG, *Betrayed by Rita Hayworth.*
The Buenos Aires Affair.
Heartbreak Tango.

RAYMOND QUENEAU, *The Last Days.*
Odile.
Pierrot Mon Ami.
Saint Glinglin.

ANN QUIN, *Berg.*
Passages.
Three.
Tripticks.

ISHMAEL REED, *The Free-Lance Pallbearers.*
The Last Days of Louisiana Red.
Ishmael Reed: The Plays.
Juice!
The Terrible Threes.
The Terrible Twos.
Yellow Back Radio Broke-Down.

JASIA REICHARDT, *15 Journeys Warsaw to London.*

JOÃO UBALDO RIBEIRO, *House of the Fortunate Buddhas.*

RAINER MARIA RILKE,
The Notebooks of Malte Laurids Brigge.

JULIÁN RÍOS, *The House of Ulysses.*
Larva: A Midsummer Night's Babel.
Poundemonium.

ALAIN ROBBE-GRILLET, *Project for a Revolution in New York.*
A Sentimental Novel.

JEAN ROLIN, *The Explosion of the Radiator Hose.*

ALIX CLEO ROUBAUD, *Alix's Journal.*

JACQUES ROUBAUD, *The Form of a City Changes Faster, Alas, Than the Human Heart.*
The Great Fire of London.
Hortense in Exile.
Hortense Is Abducted.
Mathematics.

RAYMOND ROUSSEL, *Impressions of Africa.*

VEDRANA RUDAN, *Night.*

LYDIE SALVAYRE, *The Company of Ghosts.*
The Lecture.
The Power of Flies.

LUIS RAFAEL SÁNCHEZ, *Macho Camacho's Beat.*

SEVERO SARDUY, *Cobra & Maitreya.*

NATHALIE SARRAUTE, *Do You Hear Them?*
Martereau.
The Planetarium.

ARNO SCHMIDT, *Collected Novellas.*
Collected Stories.
Nobodaddy's Children.

GAIL SCOTT, *My Paris.*

JUNE AKERS SEESE, *Is This What Other Women Feel Too?*

VIKTOR SHKLOVSKY, *Bowstring.*
Literature and Cinematography.
Theory of Prose.
Third Factory.
Zoo, or Letters Not about Love.

PIERRE SINIAC, *The Collaborators.*

KJERSTI A. SKOMSVOLD, *The Faster I Walk, the Smaller I Am.*

MARKO SOSIČ, *Ballerina, Ballerina.*

ANDRZEJ STASIUK, *Dukla.*
Fado.

GERTRUDE STEIN, *The Making of Americans.*
A Novel of Thank You.

GONÇALO M. TAVARES, *A Man: Klaus Klump.*
Jerusalem.

NIKANOR TERATOLOGEN, *Assisted Living.*

STEFAN THEMERSON, *Hobson's Island.*
The Mystery of the Sardine.
Tom Harris.

TAEKO TOMIOKA, *Building Waves.*

JOHN TOOMEY, *Sleepwalker.*

DUMITRU TSEPENEAG, *Hotel Europa.*
The Necessary Marriage.
Pigeon Post.
Vain Art of the Fugue.

ESTHER TUSQUETS, *Stranded.*

DUBRAVKA UGRESIC, *Lend Me Your Character.*
Thank You for Not Reading.

TOR ULVEN, *Replacement.*

MATI UNT, *Brecht at Night.*
Diary of a Blood Donor.
Things in the Night.

ÁLVARO URIBE & OLIVIA SEARS, EDS., *Best of Contemporary Mexican Fiction.*

ELOY URROZ, *Friction.*
The Obstacles.

LUISA VALENZUELA, *Dark Desires and the Others.*
He Who Searches.

BORIS VIAN, *Heartsnatcher.*

LLORENÇ VILLALONGA, *The Dolls' Room.*

ORNELA VORPSI, *The Country Where No One Ever Dies.*

DIANE WILLIAMS, *Excitability: Selected Stories.*
Romancer Erector.

MARGUERITE YOUNG, *Angel in the Forest.*
Miss MacIntosh, My Darling.

REYOUNG, *Unbabbling.*

VLADO ŽABOT, *The Succubus.*

ZORAN ŽIVKOVIĆ, *Hidden Camera.*

LOUIS ZUKOFSKY, *Collected Fiction.*

VITOMIL ZUPAN, *Minuet for Guitar.*

SCOTT ZWIREN, *God Head.*

AND MORE . . .